REFLEXIVE TEMA AND GLOBAL ELSEWHERES...

TEMA UND SEINE GLOBALEN WIDER-SPIEGELUNGEN ...

REFLEXIVE TEMA AND GLOBAL ELSEWHERES...
TEMA UND SEINE GLOBALEN WIDERSPIEGELUNGEN ...

FOREWORD

Kwasi Ohene-Ayeh

VORWORT

In 2021, I was invited to contribute to the long-term research project *Decolonizing Socialism: Entangled Internationalism*, which explores art, architecture, and cybernetics as distinct, yet interrelated, registers through which to reflect on East-South alliances with the German Democratic Republic (GDR) dating back to the Cold War era. It was under such auspices that I was granted a fellowship by the Van Abbemuseum in Eindhoven, Netherlands, to conceive the Ghana case study titled *Reflexive Tema and Global Elsewheres . . .* that same year. I then formed a core team comprised of colleagues such as Ato Annan, Kelvin Haizel, Ibrahim Mahama, and Isaac Abbey (aka Abbey IT-A). Our case study has yielded a diverse body of audiovisual, literary, and scholarly materials, as well as ephemera gathered from archival, institutional, and private sources.

Reflexive Tema and Global Elsewheres . . . looks into the connections between Nkrumaism, socialist internationalism, and tropical modernist architecture. It is focused on the sixtieth anniversary of Ghana's First Republic (1960–66) and begins with the establishment of the Government Printing Press, Tema, in 1964, which embodied the socialist ethos of Kwame Nkrumah's postwar agenda of emancipation and industrialization.[1] It investigates the role played by this state-run printing press in Nkrumah's post-independence vision of an African revolution whose ultimate goal would be the Continental Union Government of Africa. Also of relevance to the study is the implicit dimension of architecture[2]—how the formalist (International Style) architectural canon (which has its birthing pangs in the German Bauhaus design movement/school), socialist architecture, and Tropical Modernism implemented by British exponents in West Africa, notably Maxwell Fry and Jane Drew, came to feature in Ghana's post-independence future inaugurated in 1957 amidst the stultifying fictions of Cold War politics.

The coastal town of Tema, created to serve as the commercial and industrial heart of Ghana, is located along the Atlantic coast.[3] It is approximately 35 kilometers southeast of the capital city, Accra. According to Joe Mainoo—then chairman of the Tema Development Corporation[4]—Tema is "the first

1. Kwame Nkrumah (1909–1972) was a politician, political theorist, and pan-Africanist revolutionary who was prime minister of the Gold Coast from 1952 until 1957. He went on to become the first president of Ghana after independence in 1957. He is considered to be the "founder" of Ghana.

2. For more on the architectural dimension of the project, see *Decoso Meeting #3: Reflexive Tema and Global Elsewheres ...*, research presentation by Ato Annan and Kwasi Ohene-Ayah, posted January 9, 2022, by Decolonizing Socialism, YouTube, https://www.youtube.com/watch?v=j7yU88_Vdb0.

3. Keith Jopp, *Tema: Ghana's New Town and Harbour* (Ministry of Information, Accra, 1961), 23.

4. Now Tema Development Company Limited, TDC, "was set up in 1952 by an Act of Parliament with the sole responsibility to plan and develop about 63 square miles of public land for various land cases and also manage the township that had been created to provide accommodation to those that would be engaged in these economic operations." "About Us: Background," TDC Ghana Ltd, accessed December 16, 2024, http://tdc.gov.gh/index.htm.

2021 erhielt ich die Einladung, mich an dem Forschungsprojekt „Decolonizing Socialism: Entangled Internationalism" zu beteiligen. Dieses Projekt untersucht Künste, Architektur und Kybernetik als eigenständige, aber miteinander verschränkte Register, um durch sie Ost-Süd-Allianzen mit der Deutschen Demokratischen Republik (DDR) in Zeiten des Kalten Krieges zu reflektieren. In diesem Kontext wurde mir im selben Jahr ein Stipendium des Van Abbemuseums in Eindhoven gewährt, um unter dem Titel *Reflexive Tema and Global Elsewheres* ... (*Tema und seine globalen Widerspiegelungen* ...) eine Fallstudie zu Ghana durchzuführen. Daraufhin stellte ich ein Kernteam zusammen, dem Ato Annan, Kelvin Haizel, Ibrahim Mahama und Isaac Abbey (alias Abbey IT-A) angehörten. Unsere Fallstudie hat ein vielfältiges Korpus audiovisueller, literarischer und wissenschaftlicher Materialien hervorgebracht, ebenso gehören dazu ephemere Dokumente und Objekte aus archivalischen, institutionellen und privaten Quellen.

Tema und seine globalen Widerspiegelungen ... geht den Verbindungen zwischen Nkrumaismus, sozialistischem Internationalismus und der Architektur der Tropischen Moderne nach. Das Projekt konzentriert sich auf die sechs Jahre der ersten Republik in Ghana (1960–1966) und setzt ein mit der 1964 erfolgten Gründung der ersten staatlichen Druckerei, der Tema Printing Press, die das sozialistische Ethos von Kwame Nkrumahs Nachkriegsagenda der Emanzipation und Industrialisierung verkörperte.[1] Es untersucht die Rolle, die diese staatlich geführte Druckerei für die von Nkrumah im Anschluss an die Erlangung der Unabhängigkeit formulierte Vision einer afrikanischen Revolution spielte, deren ultimatives Ziel die politische Kontinentalunion Afrika war. Für das Projekt ebenfalls von Bedeutung ist die implizite Dimension der Architektur[2] – wie sich der formalistische Architekturkanon (des International Style, dessen Geburtswehen die Designbewegung / Schule des Bauhaus in Deutschland waren), die sozialistische Architektur und die von britischen Vertreter·innen in Westafrika, insbesondere von Maxwell Fry und Jane Drew, eingeführte Tropische Moderne eingefügt haben in die mit der Unabhängigkeit Ghanas eröffnete Zukunft, die ihren Anfang 1957 inmitten der lähmenden Fiktionen der Politik des Kalten Krieges nahm.

Die Küstenstadt Tema, geschaffen, um als gewerbliches und industrielles Herz Ghanas zu fungieren, liegt an der Atlantikküste, etwa 35 Kilometer südöstlich der Hauptstadt Accra.[3] Folgt

1. Kwame Nkrumah (1909–1972) war ein Politiker, Theoretiker und pan-afrikanistischer Revolutionär, der von 1952 bis 1957 das Amt des Premierministers der Goldküste innehatte. Nach der Erlangung der Unabhängigkeit des Landes wurde er 1957 der erste Präsident von Ghana. Er gilt als „Gründer" von Ghana.

2. Für einen tieferen Einblick in die architektonische Dimension des Projekts siehe *Decoso Meeting #3: Reflexive Tema and Global Elsewheres*, Präsentation von Ato Annan und Kwasi Ohene-Ayah, gepostet am 9. Januar 2022 von Decolonizing Socialism, YouTube, https://www.youtube.com/watch?v=j7yU88_Vdb0

3. Keith Jopp, *Tema: Ghana's New Town and Harbour*, Accra: Ministry of Information 1961, S. 23.

new town in the tropics attached to a harbour ever to be built."[5] Tema was transformed from being an agrarian and small-scale fishing economy to playing a substantial role in Nkrumah's plans for self-determination when his political party, the Convention People's Party (CPP), won a significant majority of votes in Ghana's first general elections in 1951.

This research edition montages the fragmented and incomplete story of the Tema Printing Press through factographic materials (archival resources in the form of reports, memos, letters, maps, newspaper clippings, drawings, photos, videos, audios, etc.) and memory fictions (anecdotes, interviews, artistic interventions, etc.) that we have compiled and created. It is our hope to advance this particular discourse by creating a publicly accessible online repository with all the materials generated up to this point so that publics can continue to engage with the study. These are early forays into complex geopolitical narratives of emancipation, hopelessness, resistance, and affirmative politics that begin with Ghana's and the GDR's global entanglements. This publication also features an artistic intervention in the form of Annan's digital collages, titled *Fragments of Nationhood* (2024), which were inspired by explorations in the Münzkabinett (Coin Cabinet) of the Staatliche Kunstsammlungen Dresden (Dresden State Art Collections, SKD).

We are grateful to the following collaborators in Ghana, Germany, and elsewhere in the world whose invaluable knowledge, experience, and insights helped us shape the project: Prof. John Owusu Addo, Elizabeth Asafo Adjei, Prof. Esi Sutherland Addy, Prof. S. O. Afram, Harriet Mercy Agbokah, Nick Aikens, Gilbert Amegatcher, Andrea-Vicky Amankwaa-Birago, King Ampaw, Adjoa Armah, Dr. Desmond Aryee-Boi, Roger Bekoe-Dawson, Elolo Bosoka, Nii Boye, Memory Biwa, Kojo Derban, Kodwo Eshun, Nana Kwasi Gyan-Apenteng, Michael Gyimah, Katja Hoffmann, Prof. Wilhelm Hollstein, Dr. Yaw Mantey Jectey-Nyarko, Kojo Safo Kantanka, Dr. Sylvia Karges, Lama El Khatib, Allottey Bruce Konuah, Robert Machiri, Prof. Doreen Mende, Zohra Opoku, Jasmina Al Qaisi, Ricarda Rivoir, Elisabeth Schmidt, Jihan El Tahri, and Océane Vé-Réveillac.

Further thanks go to the following institutions for their support: the Swiss National Science Foundation, Van Abbemuseum, Staatliche Kunstsammlungen Dresden (SKD), Ghana's Public Records and Archives Administration Department (PRAAD), the Information Services Department of Ghana (ISD), blaxTARLINES KUMASI, the Foundation for Contemporary Art–Ghana, Tema Development Company Limited (TDC), the *Daily Graphic*, the *Ghanaian Times*, the Ghana

5. Joseph Mainoo, letter to Kwame Nkrumah (with Tema Development Corporation letterhead), March 19, 1960.

man Joe Mainoo – damals Vorsitzender der Tema Development Corporation[4] –, ist Tema „die erste jemals in den Tropen gebaute neue Stadt, die an einen Seehafen angeschlossen ist".[5] Tema wurde von einer auf Landwirtschaft und Kleinfischerei beruhenden Wirtschaftsstruktur zu einer Schlüsselregion in Nkrumahs Plänen für die Selbstbestimmung des Landes umgewandelt, als seine politische Partei, die Convention People's Party (CPP) 1951 bei den ersten allgemeinen Wahlen in Ghana die große Mehrheit der Stimmen erhielt.

Diese Forschungsedition montiert eine fragmentierte und unvollständige Geschichte der Tema Printing Press aus faktografischen Materialien (Archivquellen in Form von Berichten, Memos, Briefen, Karten, Zeitungsausschnitten, Zeichnungen, Fotos, Videos, Audioaufnahmen und so weiter) und Erinnerungsfiktionen (Anekdoten, Interviews, künstlerische Interventionen und so weiter), die wir gesammelt und erstellt haben. Es ist unsere Hoffnung, diesen besonderen Diskurs durch die Schaffung eines öffentlich zugänglichen Online-Repositoriums mit allen bis dato generierten Materialien fortzuführen, damit sich auch weiterhin Interessierte mit dem Forschungsprojekt auseinandersetzen können. Dies sind erste Vorstöße in komplexe geopolitische Narrative der Emanzipation, der Hoffnungslosigkeit, des Widerstands und einer affirmativen Politik, die damit beginnen, dass Ghana und die DDR globale Verflechtungen eingegangen sind. In dieser Publikation findet sich auch eine künstlerische Intervention in Form von Annans digitalen Collagen mit dem Titel *Fragments of Nationhood* (Fragmente nationaler Identität, 2024), die von Erkundungen im Münzkabinett der Staatlichen Kunstsammlungen Dresden (SKD) inspiriert worden sind.

Wir danken den folgenden Mitstreiter·innen in Ghana, Deutschland und anderswo auf der Welt, deren Wissen, Erfahrungen und Einsichten uns bei der Entwicklung des Projekts unschätzbare Dienste geleistet haben: Prof. John Owusu Addo, Elizabeth Asafo Adjei, Prof. Esi Sutherland Addy, Prof. S. O. Afram, Harriet Mercy Agbokah, Nick Aikens, Gilbert Amegatcher, Andrea-Vicky Amankwaa-Birago, King Ampaw, Adjoa Armah, Dr. Desmond Aryee-Boi, Roger Bekoe-Dawson, Elolo Bosoka, Nii Boye, Memory Biwa, Kojo Derban, Kodwo Eshun, Nana Kwasi Gyan-Apenteng, Michael Gyimah, Katja Hoffmann, Prof. Dr. Wilhelm Hollstein, Dr. Yaw Mantey Jectey-Nyarko, Kojo Safo Kantanka, Dr. Sylvia Karges, Lama El Khatib, Allotey Bruce Konuah, Robert Machiri, Prof. Dr. Doreen Mende, Zohra Opoku, Jasmina Al-Qaisi, Ricarda Rivoir,

4. Heute Tema Development Company Limited. TDC „wurde 1952 durch einen Beschluss des Parlaments gegründet und hatte die einzige Aufgabe, etwa 63 Quadratmeilen öffentlichen Landes für verschiedene Zwecke zu planen und zu entwickeln und auch die Siedlung zu verwalten, die geschaffen wurde, um diejenigen unterzubringen, die in die Umsetzung dieser wirtschaftlichen Operationen eingebunden waren". „About Us: Background", TDC Ghana Ltd, http://tdc.gov.gh/index.htm

5. Joseph Mainoo, Brief an Kwame Nkrumah (auf Briefpapier der Tema Development Corporation), 19. März 1960.

National Fire Service, the National Museum, Ghana, and Assembly Press, Ghana.

A BRIEF POLITICAL-HISTORICAL CONTEXTUALIZATION

By 1961, the government of the Republic of Ghana had signed trade, cultural, and economic agreements with the government of the German Democratic Republic (GDR). The contracts covered such things as mutual long-term trade, long-term payments, and scientific, technical, and cultural cooperation agreements with the aim of strengthening bilateral relations in the areas of education, science, technology, literature, theater, music, fine art, and import and export trade (commercial and noncommercial). Similar agreements had been signed that same year between Ghana and other socialist countries in eastern Europe including Poland, Hungary, the USSR, Czechoslovakia, and Yugoslavia. The Tema Press was realized as part of this broader industrialization and Non-Aligned strategy for self-determination.[6]

Construction for the now-extinct Tema Printing Press, executed under the Ministry of Information and Broadcasting, commenced in 1962 on the heels of Nkrumah's Seven-Year Development Plan (1963/64–1969/70), conceived by the CPP that same year. According to Nkrumah, this plan was the first comprehensive economic plan ever drawn up for Ghana's development after a thorough examination of the country's needs and resources.[7] The Seven-Year Development Plan was a modern industrialist program approved by parliament in 1964 that served as the national blueprint for social and economic development during Ghana's First Republic and beyond.[8] Its utopian aims were to provide education for all children, in addition to eradicating poverty and illiteracy while improving social services, transportation, communications, and the electricity and water supply by the tenth anniversary of the Republic in 1970.[9]

Needless to say, this emancipatory project was truncated by the counter-revolutionary coup d'état which deposed Nkrumah, backed by the

6. The Non-Aligned Movement (NAM)—founded in 1961 in Belgrade, Serbia, and headquartered in Jakarta, Indonesia—formed part of the decolonial and resistance politics in developing countries that rejected the binarism of Cold War aggression. Nkrumah played a central role in its creation. The founding nations are Ghana, Egypt, Yugoslavia, Indonesia, and India.

7. *Seven-Year Plan for National Reconstruction and Development: Financial Years 1963/64–1969/70* (Office of the Planning Commission, Accra, 1964), ix.

8. Besides the comprehensive Seven-Year Plan, there were also Annual Development Plans that were used to track the "quantitative progress made so far in the implementation of the Plan and present definite programmes of action in the public sector." Ibid., 7. The first of these annual plans was drawn up in 1964.

9. Ibid., v–vi.

Elisabeth Schmidt, Jihan El-Tahri und Océane Vé-Réveillac.

Ein weiterer Dank gilt den folgenden Institutionen für ihre Unterstützung: Schweizerischer Nationalfonds, Van Abbemuseum, Staatliche Kunstsammlungen Dresden (SKD), Public Records and Archives Administration Department (PRAAD), Ghana, Information Services Department of Ghana (ISD), blaxTARLINES KUMASI, Foundation for Contemporary Art – Ghana, Tema Development Company Limited (TDC), *Daily Graphic*, *Ghanaian Times*, Ghana National Fire Service, National Museum, Ghana, und Assembly Press, Ghana.

EINE KURZE POLITISCH-HISTORISCHE EINORDNUNG

1961 hatte die Regierung der Republik Ghana mit der Regierung der Deutschen Demokratischen Republik (DDR) bereits Abkommen über Handel, Kultur und Wirtschaft abgeschlossen. Die Verträge beinhalteten Vereinbarungen zu langfristigen wechselseitigen Handelsbeziehungen und Zahlungen sowie zur wissenschaftlichen, technischen und kulturellen Zusammenarbeit. Damit wurde das Ziel verfolgt, die bilateralen Beziehungen in den Bereichen Bildung, Wissenschaft, Technologie, Literatur, Theater, Musik, bildende Künste sowie des kommerziellen und nichtkommerziellen Import- und Exporthandels zu stärken. Im selben Jahr waren ähnliche Abkommen zwischen Ghana und weiteren sozialistischen Ländern in Osteuropa geschlossen worden, darunter Polen, Ungarn, die UdSSR, die Tschechoslowakei und Jugoslawien. Die Druckerei von Tema wurde als Teil dieser umfassenderen Strategie der Industrialisierung und Blockfreiheit zur Sicherung der Selbstbestimmung realisiert.[6]

Die Bauarbeiten für die heute nicht mehr existierende Tema Printing Press, ausgeführt unter Regie des Ministeriums für Information und Rundfunk, begannen 1962, kurz nach der Verabschiedung von Nkrumahs Sieben-Jahres-Entwicklungsplan (1963/64–1969/70), der von der CPP im selben Jahr aufgestellt worden war. Nkrumah zufolge war dies der erste umfassende Wirtschaftsplan, der überhaupt jemals für Ghana entworfen wurde, nach einer umfassenden Begutachtung der Bedürfnisse und Ressourcen des Landes.[7] Der Sieben-Jahres-Entwicklungsplan war ein modernes Industrieprogramm, das 1964 vom Parlament gebilligt wurde und als nationale Blaupause für die gesellschaftliche und

6. Die Bewegung der Blockfreien Staaten (englisch *Non-Aligned Movement*, NAM) – 1961 im serbischen Belgrad gegründet und mit Hauptquartier in Jakarta, Indonesien – bildete einen Teil der dekolonialen und Widerstandspolitik in sich entwickelnden Ländern, die die aggressive binäre Spaltung des Kalten Krieges ablehnten. Nkrumah spielte bei ihrer Etablierung eine zentrale Rolle. Die Gründungsnationen sind Ghana, Ägypten, Jugoslawien, Indonesien und Indien.

7. *Seven-Year Plan for National Reconstruction and Development: Financial Years 1963/64–1969/70*, Accra: Office of the Planning Commission 1964, S. ix.

US Central Intelligence Agency in 1966[10]—two years after the adoption and implementation of the Plan by parliament.[11] But the materialist core of the Plan set out to lay the foundations for "the complete transformation of Ghana into a strong, industrialised socialist economy and society" in keeping with the ultimate aim of African unity.[12] The tripartite mission of the Plan was to completely eradicate the colonial structure of Ghana's economy; to speed up the rate of growth of the economy; and to enable a socialist transformation of Ghana's economy.[13]

The Ghana National Construction Corporation (GNCC) was responsible for building and furnishing the Tema Printing Press in 1962[14]—in addition to completing 153 houses in Tema Community 5 the following year.[15] Permits were also issued for the execution of other government projects in Tema such as the Cocoa Processing Factory and the Textile Mill—both under the Ministry of Industries[16]—an aluminum smelter, and the Accra–Tema freeway in 1962.[17] The mechanized press—equipped to handle intertype, monotype, chemigraphy, hand composing, and much more[18]—was designed by consultants and engineers of Polygraph Export GmbH. Tema Press was part of a nationwide network of government printers (State Publishing Corporation) that published, printed, and distributed educational materials as well as government stationery, including parliamentary Hansards, receipt books, vouchers, train tickets, and much more.[19] The first phase of the construction—which comprised execution of the earthworks, lavatories, dressing rooms, and garages—was authorized on July 20, 1962. Work begun on July 27 of that year, and this phase was due for completion within five calendar months from the date the tender was approved

10. Kwame Nkrumah, *Dark Days in Ghana* (Panaf, 1968)

11. There were subsequent Development Plans outlined in the different military and democratic regimes after the 1966 coup. Some sought to build on Nkrumah's, while others abandoned it. "After a series of crises and inflation," between 1966 and 1968—in the aftermath of the coup which deposed Nkrumah—a provisional "short-term" Two-Year Development Plan (mid-1968 to mid-1970), "conceived as a forerunner to a more comprehensive development plan," was implemented by the military regime of the day, the National Liberation Council, as it prepared to transition to civilian rule in 1969. National Liberation Council, *Two-Year Development Plan from Stabilisation to Development: A Plan for the Period Mid-1968 to Mid-1970* (National Liberation Council, Accra, 1968), 1–1A.

12. *Seven-Year Plan* (see n. 7), vi.

13. Ibid., ix.

14. "Tema Press: Physical Proof of Ghana's Industrialisation," *The Evening News*, September 26, 1964, 1 and 5.

15. *Monthly Report, June 1963* (Accra-Tema Development Corporation [Tema Branch], 1963), 2.

16. *Monthly Report, May 1963* (Accra-Tema Development Corporation [Tema Branch], 1963), 1.

17. *Seven-Year Plan* (see n. 7), xxii.

18. "Tema Press" (see n. 14), 3.

19. Roger Bekoe-Dawson, interview with Ato Annan, May 27, 2021.

wirtschaftliche Entwicklung während Ghanas erster Republik und darüber hinaus diente.[8] Seine Ziele waren utopisch: Schulbildung für alle Kinder, dazu die völlige Beseitigung von Armut und Analphabetismus, gleichzeitig eine Verbesserung von öffentlicher Wohlfahrt, Transportwesen, Kommunikationsinfrastruktur, Elektrizitäts- und Wasserversorgung bis zum zehnten Jahrestag der Republik im Jahr 1970.[9]

Ganz offensichtlich ist dieses emanzipatorische Projekt durch den konterrevolutionären, von der CIA unterstützen Staatsstreich, mit dem Nkrumah 1966 gestürzt wurde, abgewürgt worden[10] – zwei Jahre nach der Verabschiedung und Einführung des Plans durch das Parlament.[11] Aber in seinem materialistischen Kern war der Plan darauf angelegt, die Grundlagen zu schaffen für „die vollständige Transformation Ghanas in eine starke, industrialisierte sozialistische Ökonomie und Gesellschaft" und befand sich damit im Einklang mit dem ultimativen Ziel einer afrikanischen Einheit.[12] Die dreigeteilte Mission des Plans war die völlige Beseitigung der kolonialen Strukturen in Ghanas Wirtschaft, die Beschleunigung der wirtschaftlichen Wachstumsrate und die Ermöglichung einer sozialistischen Transformation von Ghanas Wirtschaft.[13]

Verantwortlich für den Bau und die Ausstattung der Tema Printing Press war 1962 die Ghana National Construction Corporation (GNCC)[14] – zusätzlich zur Errichtung von 153 Häusern in der Tema Community 5 im darauffolgenden Jahr.[15] Zudem wurden Genehmigungen erteilt für die Ausführung weiterer Regierungsprojekte in Tema wie etwa eine Kakaoverarbeitungsfabrik und eine Textilfabrik – beide unter Führung des Industrieministeriums[16] –, eine Aluminiumhütte und die Schnellstraße zwischen

8. Neben dem umfassenden Siebenjahresplan gab es auch jährliche Entwicklungspläne, die dazu verwendet wurden, die „bisher gemachten quantitativen Fortschritte bei der Umsetzung des Plans abzubilden und konkrete Handlungsprogramme im öffentlichen Sektor vorzulegen". *Seven-Year Development Plan: Annual Plan for the Second Plan Year, 1965 Financial Year*, Accra: Office of the Planning Commission 1965, S. 7. Der erste dieser Jahrespläne wurde 1964 erstellt.

9. *Seven-Year Plan*, S. v–vi.

10. Kwame Nkrumah, *Dark Days in Ghana*, London: Panaf 1968.

11. Es gab nachfolgende Entwicklungspläne, die unter den verschiedenen Militärregimen und demokratischen Regierungen nach dem Putsch von 1966 ausgearbeitet wurden. Einige versuchten auf dem Plan von Nkrumah aufzubauen, während andere ihn fallen ließen. „Nach einer Reihe von Krisen und steigender Inflation" zwischen 1966 und 1968 – während der Nachwehen des Putsches, der Nkrumah zu Fall brachte – wurde vom damaligen Militärregime, dem National Liberation Council, das sich auf den Übergang zur Zivilregierung im Jahr 1969 vorbereitete, ein vorläufiger „kurzfristiger" Zwei-Jahres-Plan (Mitte 1968 bis Mitte 1970) in Kraft gesetzt, der als „Vorläufer eines umfassenderen Entwicklungsplans gedacht war". National Liberation Council, *Two-Year Development Plan from Stabilisation to Development: A Plan for the Period Mid-1968 to Mid-1970*, Accra: National Liberation Council 1968, S. 1–1A.

12. *Seven-Year Plan*, S. vi.

13. Ebd., S. ix.

14. „Tema Press: Physical Proof of Ghana's Industrialisation", in: *The Evening News*, 26. September 1964, S. 1 und S. 5.

15. *Monthly Report, June 1963*, Tema: Accra-Tema Development Corporation [Tema Branch] 1963, S. 2.

16. *Monthly Report, May 1963*, Tema: Accra-Tema Development Corporation [Tema Branch] 1963, S. 1.

(which was on December 27, 1962). The project was supervised by a team of East German engineers and consultants acting under the Ministry of Information and Broadcasting. Phase two began on October 1, 1962, and was scheduled to last for twenty months with May 31, 1964, earmarked as the official date of completion. Nkrumah personally inspected and opened the Tema Press to the public on Friday, September 25, 1964, at a ceremony which was attended by then Deputy Prime Minister of the GDR, Paul Scholz.[20] Decrying the "slow-moving" pace of the British colonial government to establish any meaningful printing industry in the Gold Coast (the colonial precursor of the nation-state Ghana) since 1857, Ashford Emmanuel Inkumsah, then Minister of Information and Broadcasting, boasted that the Tema Press was "physical proof of the high tempo of the planned industrialization of [Ghana], and evidence of the sense of urgency with which we are determined to implement the Seven-Year Development Plan."[21]

In a letter received from Assembly Press[22]—the only existing institution among the government printers located in Accra which has now been divested—we were informed by the managing director that the "Tema Press was placed under the divestiture programme and subsequently transferred to the Divestiture Implementation Committee (DIC), which had been absorbed by the State Interests and Governance Authority (SIGA)."[23] This phenomenon can be traced back to Ghana's economic recovery program, launched seventeen years after Nkrumah's overthrow owing to Ghana's adoption of neoliberal economic policies via the so-called Structural Adjustment Program (SAP) in the form of debt instruments doled out by the International Monetary Fund (IMF) and the World Bank.[24] The SAP proceeded to radically limit any extensive government involvement in the economy and opened it up to the "free market orthodoxy." A few of the overall effects of SAP on Ghana's economy were felt through policies that caused 1) currency devaluation against the US

20. "Tema Press" (see n. 14), 3.

21. Ibid. Inkumsah recounted how the colonial government signed an order for a printing machine from the United Kingdom in 1857 which took seventeen years to actually be installed in the Gold Coast. He further noted that the first Monotype apparatus was installed in the Gold Coast in 1907, five years after the first Government Printer was appointed.

22. Assembly Press, which was one of the government printers located in Accra, was "converted into a Limited Liability Company under the Statutory Corporations (Conversion to Companies) Act 461, 1993, and renamed Ghana Publishing Company Limited in 2007." "GPLC – About Us," Ghana Publishing Company Limited, accessed December 16, 2024, https://www.ghanapublishing.com/index.php/about-us.

23. David Boateng Asante, letter to Ato Annan and Kwasi Ohene-Ayeh, September 8, 2021.

24. *Ghana-Enhanced Structural Adjustment Facility: Economic and Financial Policy Framework Paper*, International Monetary Fund, accessed December 16, 2024, https://www.imf.org/external/np/pfp/ghana/ghana0.htm.

Accra und Tema 1962.[17] Die maschinelle Druckerei – ausgestattet mit Intertype- und Monotype-Setzmaschinen, Maschinen für chemigrafische Verfahren, Handsatz und vieles mehr[18] – war von Beratern und Ingenieuren der Polygraph Export GmbH entworfen worden. Die Tema Press war Teil eines landesweiten Netzwerks von staatlichen Druckereien (State Publishing Corporation), das Lehrmaterialien verlegte, druckte und vertrieb und auch Druckerzeugnisse für die Regierung und Verwaltung produzierte, darunter Parlamentsprotokolle, Quittungsblöcke, Coupons, Zugfahrkarten und vieles andere mehr.[19] Die erste Bauphase – die die Ausführung der Erdaushubarbeiten, der Sanitäranlagen, Umkleideräume und Garagen umfasste – wurde am 20. Juli 1962 bewilligt. Die Arbeiten begannen am 27. Juli des Jahres und der Abschluss dieser Arbeiten war innerhalb von fünf Kalendermonaten nach Erteilung des Auftrags vorgesehen (also zum 27. Dezember 1962). Das Projekt wurde beaufsichtigt durch ein Team von Ingenieuren und Beratern aus der DDR, die im Auftrag des Ministeriums für Information und Rundfunk agierten. Phase 2 begann am 1. Oktober 1962 und sollte laut Plan 20 Monate dauern, als offizielles Fertigstellungsdatum war der 31. Mai 1964 vermerkt. Nkrumah höchstselbst inspizierte die Tema Press und übergab sie am Freitag, den 25. September 1964 mit einer Zeremonie der Öffentlichkeit, an der auch der stellvertretende Vorsitzende des Ministerrates der DDR, Paul Scholz, teilnahm.[20] Ashford Emmanuel Inkumsah, der Minister für Information und Rundfunk, beklagte das geringe Tempo, mit dem die britische Kolonialregierung seit 1857 an der Goldküste (dem kolonialen Vorläufer des Nationalstaats Ghana) eine nennenswerte Druckindustrie aufgebaut hatte, und rühmte die Tema Press als „physischen Beweis für das hohe Tempo der geplanten Industrialisierung [Ghanas] und als Beleg für die Dringlichkeit, mit der wir entschlossen sind, den Sieben-Jahres-Entwicklungsplan umzusetzen".[21]

In einem Schreiben der Assembly Press[22] – der einzigen in Accra ansässigen staatlichen Druckerei, die bis heute besteht, inzwischen aber veräußert wurde – teilte uns der Geschäftsführer mit, dass die „Tema Press dem Veräußerungsprogramm unterstellt und anschließend dem Divestiture Implementation Committee (DIC) übertragen wurde, das derzeit von der State Interests

17. *Seven-Year Plan*, S. xxii.

18. „Tema Press", S. 3.

19. Roger Bekoe-Dawson im Gespräch mit Ato Annan, 27. Mai 2021.

20. „Tema Press", S. 3.

21. Ebd. Inkumsah schilderte, wie die Kolonialverwaltung im Jahr 1857 eine Bestellung für eine Druckerpresse aus dem Vereinigten Königreich unterzeichnet hatte, die erst nach 17 Jahren tatsächlich an der Goldküste installiert wurde. Weiterhin stellte er fest, dass die erste Monotype-Setzmaschine 1907 in der Goldküste aufgestellt wurde, fünf Jahre nachdem der erste staatliche Drucker ernannt worden war.

22. Assembly Press, eine der ersten in Accra angesiedelten staatlichen Druckereien, wurde „2007 in eine Limited Liability Company unter dem Statutory Corporations (Conversion to Companies) Act 461 von 1993 umgewandelt und umbenannt in Ghana Publishing Company Limited". „GPLC – About Us", Ghana Publishing Company Limited, https://www.ghanapublishing.com/index.php/about-us

dollar, providing a deregulatory framework that significantly benefited private-sector participation in the economy—for example, the passing of the Statutory Corporations Act in 1995 which converted public corporations into companies ripe for privatization; 2) policies to be implemented that accelerated divesture—between 1993 and 1997, the government of Ghana divested a total of 48 state-owned enterprises from a list of 110; 3) financial liberalization—two of the biggest publicly owned commercial banks, the Social Security Bank (SSB[25]) and the Ghana Commercial Bank (GCB), were privatized such that "majority share holdings in SSB passed into private hands in 1996 with foreign strategic investors obtaining management control";[26] and 4) petroleum deregulation and public service reforms.

In sum, the World Bank has, since the early 1980s, embedded itself in the Ghanaian economy by "assisting" the government of Ghana in the implementation of an expenditure control system; the reevaluation of spending priorities in the social sectors; the development of a public service restructuring plan, including identifying areas for the downsizing of functions and employment; the implementation of VAT (Value Added Tax); banking supervision; the divestiture and privatization of parastatals; the concessioning of rail transport services and the reform of the road network management and maintenance.[27]

This exploitative debtor-creditor relationship (which leads to the universalization of debt)—to which Nkrumah was passionately and unequivocally opposed[28]—is a late twentieth-century phenomenon with consequences for the whole world.[29]

In conclusion, unconfirmed witness accounts gathered during the course of our research indicate that the press building had been ravaged by a fire in 2011. We visited the Tema Industrial Area Fire Station to verify this claim. Staff members

25. SSB was licensed to operate as a bank in 1976. By 1997, 52 percent of its shares had been bought by foreign corporations. In 2003, it became a subsidiary of Société Générale, with the French entity controlling 51 percent of its shares. The name of the bank was changed to SG-SSB. By 2016, Société Générale controlled 56.67 percent of the shareholding (see https://societegenerale.com.gh/en/your-bank/corporate-profile/history-the-bank/). The bank currently goes by the name Société Générale Ghana. The future of the bank is, however, unknown considering that after twenty years of operations, Société Générale has announced that it is ceasing its operations in Africa—Ghana, Tunisia, and Cameroon. See Kabah Atawoge, "Société Générale to Exit Ghana after 20 Years," *CNR Citi Newsroom*, May 6, 2024, https://citinewsroom.com/2024/05/societe-generale-to-exit-ghana-after-20-years/.

26. *Ghana-Enhanced Structural Adjustment Facility* (see n. 24).

27. Ibid.

28. Kwame Nkrumah, *Neo-Colonialism: The Last Stage of Imperialism* (International Publishers, 1966).

29. See Maurizio Lazzarato, *The Making of the Indebted Man: An Essay on the Neoliberal Condition* (Semiotext[e], 2012); Walter Rodney, *How Europe Underdeveloped Africa*, rev. ed. (Howard University Press, 1981).

and Governance Authority (SIGA) übernommen wurde".[23] Dieses Phänomen lässt sich auf das ghanaische Programm zur wirtschaftlichen Erholung zurückführen, das 17 Jahre nach dem Sturz Nkrumahs eingeleitet wurde, weil Ghana mit dem sogenannten Strukturanpassungsprogramm (SAP) eine neoliberale Wirtschaftspolitik verfolgte, und zwar in Form von Schuldtiteln, die vom Internationalen Währungsfonds (IWF) und der Weltbank ausgegeben wurden.[24] Das SAP schränkte jede umfassende staatliche Beteiligung an der Wirtschaft radikal ein und öffnete sie für die Orthodoxie des „freien Marktes". Einige der allgemeinen Auswirkungen des SAP auf die ghanaische Wirtschaft sind durch folgende Maßnahmen spürbar: 1) Abwertung der Währung gegenüber dem US-Dollar, Schaffung eines deregulierenden Rahmens, der die Beteiligung des Privatsektors an der Wirtschaft erheblich begünstigte – beispielsweise durch die Verabschiedung des Statutory Corporations Act im Jahr 1995, mit dem öffentliche Unternehmen in privatisierungsreife Unternehmen umgewandelt wurden; 2) Umsetzung von Maßnahmen, die die Veräußerung beschleunigten – zwischen 1993 und 1997 veräußerte die ghanaische Regierung insgesamt 48 aus einer Liste von 110 staatlichen Unternehmen; 3) finanzielle Liberalisierung – zwei der größten kommerziellen Banken in öffentlicher Hand, die Social Security Bank (SSB[25]) und die Ghana Commercial Bank (GCB), wurden privatisiert, so dass die „Mehrheit der Anteile an der SSB 1996 in private Hände überging und ausländische strategische Investoren die Kontrolle über das Management erlangten";[26] 4) Deregulierung des Ölsektors und Reformen der öffentlichen Verwaltung.

Kurz gesagt hat sich die Weltbank seit den frühen 1980er Jahren in der ghanaischen Wirtschaft eingenistet, indem sie der Regierung Ghanas „geholfen" hat bei „der Implementierung eines Ausgabenkontrollsystems; einer Neubewertung von Ausgabeprioritäten im Sozialsektor; der Entwicklung eines Restrukturierungsplans der öffentlichen Verwaltung, einschließlich der Identifizierung von Bereichen für einen Abbau von Aufgabenfeldern und Stellen; der Einführung der Mehrwertsteuer; Bankenaufsicht; der Zerschlagung und Privatisierung von halbstaatlichen

23. David Boateng Asante, Brief an Ato Annan und Kwasi Ohene-Ayeh, 8. September 2021.

24. *Ghana-Enhanced Structural Adjustment Facility: Economic and Financial Policy Framework Paper*, Internationaler Währungsfonds, https://www.imf.org/external/np/pfp/ghana/ghana0.htm

25. Die SSB erhielt 1976 die Lizenz, als Bank zu operieren. Bis 1997 waren 52 Prozent ihrer Anteile von ausländischen Unternehmen aufgekauft worden, 2003 wurde sie zu einer Tochtergesellschaft der französischen Société Générale, die 51 Prozent der Anteile kontrollierte. Der Name der Bank wurde geändert zu SG-SSB. 2016 kontrollierte die Société Générale 56,67 Prozent der Anteile (siehe https://societegenerale.com.gh/en/your-bank/corporate-profile/history-the-bank/). Die Bank trägt mittlerweile den Namen Société Générale Ghana. Die Zukunft der Bank ist jedoch ungewiss in Anbetracht der Tatsache, dass die Société Générale nach 20 Jahren geschäftlicher Tätigkeit angekündigt hat, ihre Aktivitäten in Afrika (in Ghana, Tunesien und Kamerun) einzustellen. Siehe Kabah Atawoge, „Société Générale to Exit Ghana after 20 Years", *CNR Citi Newsroom*, 6. Mai 2024, https://citinewsroom.com/2024/05/societe-generale-to-exit-ghana-after-20-years/

26. *Ghana-Enhanced Structural Adjustment Facility*.

present there confirmed that there had been a fire incident reported at the location.[30] However, attempts to explore their official records to verify the incident at the sub-divisional station (regional headquarters) of the Ghana National Fire Service in Tema Community 2 has yet to yield any concrete results. Nonetheless, the original site where the Tema Press was built is now occupied by the import/export company known as Amaris Terminal Limited. It exists as a "Public Private Partnership" between the Ghana Ports and Harbours Authority and the Jospong Group of Companies based in Ghana. Amaris Terminal Limited describes itself on Facebook and LinkedIn as a "100% Ghanaian owned company licensed by the Ghana Ports and Harbours Authority to operate as an export terminal at the port of Tema."

It is under such complex historical and contemporary geopolitical currents that we attempt to re-member the spectral Tema Press.

30. A member of the fire service whom I met on my visit to the station attested to having been one of the respondents on call that day.

Unternehmen; der Konzessionierung des Schienentransports und einer Reform von Verwaltung und Unterhalt des Schienennetzwerks".[27]

Diese ausbeuterische Schuldner-Gläubiger-Beziehung (die zu einer Universalisierung der Schulden führt) – gegen die sich Nkrumah leidenschaftlich und unmissverständlich aussprach[28] – ist ein Phänomen des späten 20. Jahrhunderts, das sich auf der ganzen Welt beobachten lässt.[29]

Unbestätigten Zeugenaussagen zufolge, die wir im Laufe unserer Recherchen gesammelt haben, wurde das verlassene Druckereigebäude 2011 durch ein Feuer verwüstet. Wir haben die Feuerwache im Industriegebiet von Tema besucht, um diese Behauptung zu überprüfen. Die dort anwesenden Mitarbeiter·innen bestätigten, dass es dort einen Brand gegeben hat.[30] Versuche, die offiziellen Unterlagen zu prüfen, um den Vorfall in der Unterbezirksstation (regionaler Hauptsitz) des Ghana National Fire Service in Tema Community 2 zu verifizieren, haben jedoch noch keine konkreten Ergebnisse gebracht. Der ursprüngliche Standort, an dem die Tema Press gebaut wurde, wird heute von dem Import- / Exportunternehmen Amaris Terminal Limited genutzt. Es handelt sich um eine „öffentlich-private Partnerschaft" zwischen der Ghana Ports and Harbours Authority und der Jospong Group of Companies mit Sitz in Ghana. Amaris Terminal Limited definiert sich auf Facebook und LinkedIn als „100% ghanaisches Unternehmen, das von der Ghana Ports and Harbours Authority eine Lizenz für den Betrieb eines Exportterminals im Hafen von Tema erhalten hat".

Vor dem Hintergrund solch komplexer historischer und aktueller geopolitischer Strömungen versuchen wir, die geisterhafte Erscheinung der Tema Press in Erinnerung zu rufen.

27. Ebd.

28. Kwame Nkrumah, *Neo-Colonialism: The Last Stage of Imperialism*, New York: International Publishers 1966.

29. Vgl. Maurizio Lazzarato, *Die Fabrik des verschuldeten Menschen – ein Essay über das neoliberale Leben*, Berlin: b_books 2012; Walter Rodney, *Wie Europa Afrika unterentwickelte*, Berlin: Manifest 2023.

30. Ein Mitglied der Feuerwehr, den ich bei meinem Besuch in der Feuerwache traf, bestätigte, dass er zu den Einsatzkräften an jenem Tag gehörte.

AMIDST THE AMBIVALENT PROMISES, THE ROSES FADED AND THE DREAMS DISAPPEARED

Ato Annan

UNTER DEN ZWIESPALTIGEN VERSPRECHUNGEN VERWELKTEN DIE ROSEN UND VERSCHWANDEN DIE TRAUME

1. Kwame Nkrumah, *I Speak of Freedom: A Statement of African Ideology* (Heinemann, 1961), 145.

2. Kwame Nkrumah, *Neo-Colonialism: The Last Stage of Imperialism* (Thomas Nelson & Sons, 1965), 13.

3. Brian Larkin, "The Politics and Poetics of Infrastructure," *Annual Review of Anthropology* 42 (2013): 327–43, here: 337.

> "We cannot tell our people that material benefits and growth and modern progress are not for them. If we do, they will throw us out and seek other leaders who promise more. And they will abandon us, too, if we do not reasonably measure and respond to their hopes."[1]

The development of infrastructure on the Gold Coast under British colonial rule was primarily designed to serve the interests of England. For instance, the railways were constructed with the main objective of transporting the Gold Coast's natural resources—such as raw gold, timber, cocoa beans, and bauxite—from the interior regions to the coast, where they were loaded onto ships bound directly for England. British rule was marked by a long history of systematic exploitation by an imperialist government. Kwame Nkrumah, Ghana's first president, summed it up in his work *Neo-Colonialism: The Last Stage of Imperialism*, stating, "Africa is a paradox. . . . Her earth is rich, yet the products that come from above and below her soil continue to enrich, not Africans predominantly, but groups and individuals who operate to Africa's impoverishment."[2] The wealth of Africa—its mineral, oil, and land resources—is well known.

THE YEAR IS 1957 . . .

After gaining independence, Nkrumah—echoing the fervent dreams of many post-independence leaders of the 1950s and 60s—embarked on an ambitious project to deliver modernity to his nascent nation. He set in motion the process for structural and institutional changes, with infrastructure playing a central role in this modernization agenda. This raises the question of why post-independence leaders embraced modernization so quickly, despite the colonial project having used it as a pretext, while failing to deliver on its promises. One way to explore this question is to speculate that Nkrumah viewed infrastructure as more than mere physical systems; he likely viewed it as a crucial cultural and social force that shapes how people experience modernity.[3] It's even plausible to argue that he considered it an essential conduit through which Ghana could connect different scales—local, national, global—in shaping political, social, and economic processes.

> „Wir können unserem Volk nicht sagen, dass materielle Vorteile und Wachstum und moderner Fortschritt nichts für sie sind. Wenn wir das tun, werden sie uns hinauswerfen und sich andere Anführer suchen, die mehr versprechen. Und sie werden uns auch fallenlassen, wenn wir nicht in vernünftiger Weise ihre Hoffnungen ermessen und auf sie reagieren."[1]

Die Entwicklung der Infrastruktur an der Goldküste unter der britischen Kolonialherrschaft war im Wesentlichen so gestaltet, dass sie den Interessen Englands diente. Beispielsweise wurden die Eisenbahnlinien mit dem Hauptzweck angelegt, die Bodenschätze und Ressourcen der Goldküste – wie Rohgold, Holz, Kakaobohnen und Bauxit – aus den Regionen im Landesinneren an die Küste zu transportieren, wo sie auf Schiffe verladen wurden, die direkt nach England steuerten. Kennzeichnend für die britische Herrschaft war eine lange Geschichte der systematischen Ausbeutung durch eine imperialistische Verwaltung. Kwame Nkrumah, der erste Präsident Ghanas, brachte das in seinem Werk *Neo-Colonialism: The Last Stage of Imperialism* in folgenden Worten auf den Punkt: „Afrika ist ein Paradox. […] Der Boden ist reich, doch die Produkte, die über und unter dem Erdboden hervorgebracht werden, bereichern keineswegs die Afrikaner·innen, sondern weiterhin hauptsächlich Gruppen und Individuen, die an der Verarmung Afrikas arbeiten."[2] Der Reichtum Afrikas – seine Mineralien, Ölvorkommen und Landressourcen – ist wohlbekannt.

WIR SCHREIBEN DAS JAHR 1957 ...

Nach der Erlangung der Unabhängigkeit nahm Nkrumah – darin den fieberhaften Träumen vieler Oberhäupter von Staaten mit frisch gewonnener Unabhängigkeit in den 1950er und 1960er Jahren nacheifernd – ein ehrgeiziges Projekt in Angriff, um sein aufstrebendes Land in die Moderne zu führen. Er setzte den Prozess der strukturellen und institutionellen Veränderungen in Gang, wobei die Infrastruktur eine zentrale Rolle in dieser Modernisierungsagenda spielte. Das wirft die Frage auf, warum die nach der Unabhängigkeit an die Macht gekommenen Politiker so schnell auf Modernisierung setzten, obwohl das koloniale Projekt genau diese doch zum Deckmantel genommen und es zugleich versäumte hatte, die damit einhergehenden Versprechungen einzulösen. Eine Möglichkeit, dieser Frage nachzugehen, ist die

1. Kwame Nkrumah, *I Speak of Freedom: A Statement of African Ideology*, London: Heinemann 1961, S. 145.

2. Kwame Nkrumah, *Neo-Colonialism: The Last Stage of Imperialism*, London: Thomas Nelson & Sons 1965, S. 13.

BUILDING NEW FUTURES ...

The idea of a new future was a negotiable act of both defiance and hope; Ghana's future would not be dictated by the remnants of colonial rule but by the vision of a nation determined to reclaim its destiny. The vehicle to carry this through was the Seven-Year Development Plan drafted in 1963. It was a plan for a radical social transformation. Contained in the plan was the expansion of education, healthcare, and industrial facilities, which was intended to create a well-rounded, self-sustaining society. Nkrumah envisioned a Ghana where every citizen could contribute to and benefit from the nation's progress—a stark contrast to the exploitative system of the colonial era, where resources flowed out of the country, leaving the people impoverished.

Building new futures within the context of the post-independent Ghana was about crafting a strategy that was both forward-looking and deeply connected to the historical experiences that had shaped the nation. It was a call to action for Ghanaians to take ownership of their destiny, innovate within their unique context, and work collaboratively to build a future that would be prosperous, equitable, and sustainable.

The black man is capable of managing his own affairs.[4]

4. Kwame Nkrumah, part of his speech at Ghana's independence ceremony, Accra, Ghana, March 6, 1957.

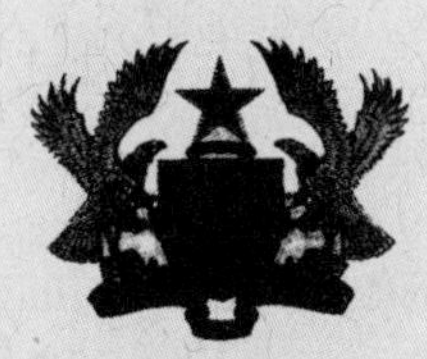

GHANA

SEVEN-YEAR DEVELOPMENT PLAN

1963/64 TO 1969/70

PRICE: TEN SHILLINGS

Vermutung, dass Nkrumah die Infrastruktur nicht bloß als rein physisches System betrachtete, sondern wahrscheinlich auch als eine entscheidende kulturelle und gesellschaftliche Triebkraft sah, die die Art und Weise prägt, in der die Menschen die Moderne erleben.[3] Es erscheint sogar plausibel, zu argumentieren, dass er sie als einen wesentlichen Brückenpfeiler begriff, durch den Ghana verschiedene Ebenen – lokaler, nationaler und globaler Art – bei der Gestaltung politischer, sozialer und wirtschaftlicher Prozesse miteinander verbinden konnte.

NEUE ZUKÜNFTE BAUEN ...

Die Idee einer neuen Zukunft war ein Akt, in dem sich Widerstandswille wie Hoffnung ausdrückten: Ghanas Zukunft sollte nicht von den Überbleibseln der Kolonialherrschaft diktiert werden, sondern von der Vision einer Nation, die entschlossen war, ihr Schicksal zurückzufordern. Das Mittel zu ihrer Durchsetzung war der 1963 entworfene Sieben-Jahres-Entwicklungsplan. Es war der Plan einer radikalen gesellschaftlichen Transformation. Dazu gehörte der Ausbau des Bildungssystems, des Gesundheitswesens und des Industriesektors, mit dem Ziel, eine ausgewogene, tragfähige Gesellschaft zu schaffen. Nkrumah schwebte ein Ghana vor, in dem jeder Bürger und jede Bürgerin zum Fortschritt der Nation beitragen und von diesem profitieren konnte – ein krasser Gegensatz zum ausbeuterischen System der Kolonialzeit, als die Bodenschätze aus dem Land flossen und eine verarmte Bevölkerung zurückließen.

3. Brian Larkin, „The Politics and Poetics of Infrastructure", in: *Annual Review of Anthropology* 42, 2013, S. 327–343, hier: S. 337.

Kwame Nkrumah, foreword to *Ghana: Seven Year Development Plan, 1963/64 to 1969/70*

FOREWORD

The Seven-year Development Plan which is now published embodies the proposals in the Party's Programme of Work and Happiness adopted at the Party Congress in July, 1962, and accepted by the country.

The Plan provides the blueprint for the future progress and development of Ghana as a nation. It is a programme of social and economic development based on the use of science and technology to revolutionize our agriculture and industry. It is designed to provide the basis not only of our national progress and prosperity, but also of our ability to contribute to the advancement of the African continent.

Our aim is to establish in Ghana a strong and progressive society in which no one will have any anxiety about the basic means of life, about work, food and shelter; where poverty and illiteracy no longer exist and disease is brought under control; and where our educational facilities provide all the children of Ghana with the best possible opportunities for the development of their potentialities.

The material basis for a socialist society can only be created by the labour of its people. This requires the highest sense of dedication on the part of all within the society. In working for the economic and social reconstruction of Ghana, we must see to it that the fruits of the people's labour shall belong to them, not to any class of exploiters. But first of all we must create the wealth. The only way to build up the national wealth is to maintain a maximum rate of productive investment in industry and agriculture.

The Plan, therefore, lays its greatest emphasis on the modernisation of agriculture and the most rapid expansion of industrial activity in Ghana. The essential aim of the Plan is to provide for all the people of Ghana who are able and willing to work, the opportunity for employment at a high level of productivity. Only in this way can the standard of living of the masses of the African people be raised to a level consistent with the human dignity of the man of the twentieth century. It must be the cardinal duty of all of us in Government, in productive enterprise and in our private lives to ensure at all times that everything is done to promote the highest level of activity in agriculture and industry.

This development must proceed in such a way as to promote our national independence and the unity of the African continent. We in Ghana have a mixed economy in which we have assigned to both public and private enterprise legitimate and important roles to play in our national development. We intend, however, to use the resources of the State to the maximum degree possible for productive investment in agriculture and industry.

FOREWORD

The Plan also provides for the development of the social services, of transport and communications, of electricity and water supplies on a scale hitherto unprecedented in Ghana. But proportionately it provides that the rate of investment in agriculture and industry and in the training of the manpower to run the economy should increase even faster.

Apart from the welfare of the individual Ghanaian, we intend to use the resources which our participation in the productive economy yields to the State to promote the economic independence of Ghana and the unity of Africa. It is therefore planned that the investments of the State in agriculture and industry should be so directed that the most strategic sectors of production will come under public control. It is also provided in the Plan that Ghana will actively participate in the movement towards Africa's economic unity as a part of the eventual unification of the continent. Only an economically strong Ghana can play a meaningful role in this historical process.

It is our hope that by the end of this Plan in December, 1970—which will coincide with the tenth anniversary of the Republic—firm foundations will have been laid for the complete transformation of Ghana into a strong, industrialised socialist economy and society.

The Plan has been prepared by the National Planning Commission under my Chairmanship, with the assistance of experts from Ghana and abroad. It sets out clearly the effort and sacrifice which will be required of each of us to enable the Plan to succeed. I, for my part, am determined that the Plan shall succeed but my determination must be supported by the combined efforts of the whole nation, including Members of Parliament, our Public Servants, our farmers and our working people.

In this spirit, I charge all of you to study this Plan very carefully and in doing so to consider what Ghana requires of you in respect of its implementation. If we all work hard and conscientiously at our tasks under this Plan, we can look forward with hope to a new Ghana where the opportunities for work and happiness will be matched by the abundant fruits of labour for all.

Kwame Nkrumah

President of the Republic of Ghana

vi

Kwame Nkrumah, Vorwort zu *Ghana: Seven Year Development Plan, 1963/64 to 1969/70*

UNEASY BEDMATES …

Nkrumah's efforts to modernize Ghana were not without their critics, both at home and abroad. The scale of his ambition, the costs involved, and the political risks he took made him a polarizing figure. Yet, he persisted and pursued his vision through strategic alliances as a means of delivering modernity and sovereignty to Ghana. However, this persistence is what the late Ali Mazrui, a prominent African scholar and political commentator, characterizes as follows: "Some African leaders have opted for a shortcut to industrialization by mortgaging their souls to Western interests. They have accepted the tools of exploitation in return for immediate economic benefits, which can ultimately undermine their countries' long-term development and independence."[5] Our current crisis may force us to give Mazrui's statement prophetic status. However, could it have underestimated the pragmatism that was required in Nkrumah's time? Was his willingness to work with Western interests a calculated risk to achieve immediate industrial and economic goals?

The significant challenges in a post-independence context, some of which included limited resources and infrastructure, presented difficult choices that had to be made in navigating these challenges. Faced with such daunting tasks, Nkrumah believed in using whatever resources were available to balance global influences, secure Ghana's development, and ultimately work toward a self-sufficient, united Africa. We can reconcile this with his involvement as a leading figure in the Non-Aligned Movement, which sought to avoid dependency on either the Western or Eastern Bloc. This was a vivid demonstration that post-independent nations could engage with the rest of the world on their own terms.

> *We face neither East nor West: we face forward.*[6]

These strategic alliances, collaborations, and partnerships, were instrumental in launching several significant industrial and infrastructure projects in Ghana. Some key results of these partnerships are as follows:

The Akosombo Dam, part of the Volta River Project. It was constructed with the collaboration of the US firm Kaiser Aluminum and received substantial

5. *The Africans: A Triple Heritage*, episode 4, "Tools of Exploitation," written and presented by Ali A. Mazrui, BBC and Public Broadcasting Service (WETA), 1986.

6. Samuel Obeng, *Selected Speeches: Kwame Nkrumah*, vol. 1. (Afram Publications, 1979), 52.

Beim Aufbau neuer Zukünfte ging es in Ghana nach der Unabhängigkeit um die Entwicklung einer nach vorne gerichteten Strategie, die zugleich eng mit den historischen Erfahrungen, die das Land geprägt haben, verbunden war. Es war ein Weckruf an die Ghanaer, ihr Schicksal in die eigene Hand zu nehmen und in ihrem einzigartigen Zusammenhang innovative Ideen zu entwickeln und gemeinsam eine prosperierende, gerechte und nachhaltige Zukunft aufzubauen.

> „Der Schwarze Mensch ist in der Lage, sich selbst um seine Angelegenheiten zu kümmern."[4]

UNBEQUEME BETTGENOSSEN …

Nkrumahs Bestrebungen zur Modernisierung Ghanas blieben nicht unwidersprochen, sowohl innerhalb des Landes wie auch international. Das Ausmaß seiner Vorhaben, die damit verbundenen Kosten und die von ihm eingegangenen politischen Risiken machten ihn zu einer polarisierenden Figur. Nichtsdestotrotz blieb er hartnäckig und verfolgte seine Vision mittels strategischer Allianzen, um Ghana zu Modernität und Souveränität zu verhelfen. Diese Beharrlichkeit charakterisierte der verstorbene prominente afrikanische Wissenschaftler und politische Kommentator Ali Mazrui allerdings mit folgenden Worten: „Einige afrikanische Staatenlenker haben eine Abkürzung auf dem Weg zur Industrialisierung gewählt, indem sie ihre Seele an westliche Interessen verpfändet haben. Sie haben für kurzfristige wirtschaftliche Vorteile die Werkzeuge der Ausbeutung akzeptiert, die letzten Endes die langfristige Entwicklung und die Unabhängigkeit ihrer Länder untergraben."[5] Die gegenwärtige Krise könnte uns dazu veranlassen, Mazruis Aussage eine prophetische Kraft zuzuschreiben. Aber hat er vielleicht den Pragmatismus unterschätzt, der zu Nkrumahs Zeiten vonnöten war? War dessen Bereitschaft, auf westliche Interessen einzugehen, ein kalkuliertes Risiko, um unmittelbare industrielle und wirtschaftliche Ziele zu erreichen?

Die erheblichen Herausforderungen in der Zeit nach der Unabhängigkeit, zu denen auch begrenzte Ressourcen und schwache oder fehlende Infrastruktur gehörten, stellten das Land vor schwierige Entscheidungen, die bei der Bewältigung dieser Herausforderungen getroffen werden mussten. Angesichts

4. Kwame Nkrumah, aus seiner Rede gehalten bei der Unabhängigkeitszeremonie Ghanas, Accra, Ghana, 6. März 1957.

5. *The Africans: A Triple Heritage*, Folge 4, „Tools of Exploitation", geschrieben und präsentiert von Ali A. Mazrui, BBC und Public Broadcasting Service (WETA) 1986.

STRICTLY CONFIDENTIAL

Report on Agreements signed with the Government of the German Democratic Republic

1. Terms of Reference:

The terms of reference of the Delegation are to negotiate and conclude Trade and Economic Agreements based on the Aide Memoire presented by Osagyefo Dr. Kwame Nkrumah to His Excellency Mr. Walter Ulbricht, President of the Council of State of the German Democratic Republic during his visit to the German Democratic Republic in August 1961.

2. Agreements concluded:

The following Agreements (copies attached) were signed on the 19th of October, 1961 :-

(a) Long-Term Trade Agreement
(b) Long-Term Payments Agreement
(c) Scientific and Technical Agreement
(d) Cultural Co-operation Agreement.

3. Summary of salient points in the Agreements:

(a) Long-Term Trade Agreement - At the discussions held in the office of the State Planning Commission of the German Democratic Republic under the chairmanship of His Excellency Karl Mewis, President of the State Planning Commission and Leader of the German Democratic Republic Delegation, it was agreed to achieve a balance in the annual value of goods mutually exchanged and to increase the annual turnover trade figures between the two countries from a level of £2.5-million in the first year to £5-million in each direction by the end of the five-year period covered by the Agreement. The German Democratic Republic side pointed out that they could not see the possibility of realising the turnover of £20-million to £25-million on each side proposed in the

/AVTM Aide ...../2

Agreements between the Government of Ghana and the Government of the German Democratic Republic, November 1, 1961

dieser gewaltigen Aufgaben setzte Nkrumah darauf, alle verfügbaren Ressourcen zu nutzen, um globale Einflüsse auszugleichen, die Entwicklung Ghanas zu sichern und letztlich auf ein autarkes, geeintes Afrika hinzuarbeiten. Das steht durchaus im Einklang mit seinem Engagement als führende Persönlichkeit in der Bewegung der Blockfreien Staaten, die eine Abhängigkeit vom westlichen wie vom östlichen Block vermeiden wollte. Es war ein anschaulicher Beweis dafür, dass die unabhängig gewordenen Nationen mit dem Rest der Welt zu ihren eigenen Bedingungen verkehren konnten.

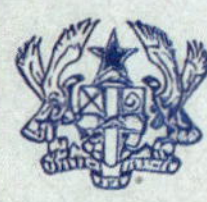

2.

Aide Memoire. In this regard, I have to draw attention to the attached exchanged letters regarding the quantity of Cocoa which the German Democratic Republic will wish to purchase from Ghana. Between 8,000 tons and 12,000 tons of Cocoa Beans will be purchased annually depending on the balance of trade between the two countries as compared with the proposed purchase of 20,000 tons to 25,000 tons annually indicated in the Aide Memoire.

(b) Long-Term Payments Agreement - With regard to the question of credit facilities for purchases made under the Trade Agreement to enable repayment over the period of five to six years, the German Democratic Republic side explained that their economy was heavily committed to their own internal re-construction programme, and could not therefore make any offer at this stage, but would be prepared to review the matter after one year.

(c) Cultural Co-operation Agreement - Particular attention is drawn to Item 27 of Appendix "C" of the Aide Memoire for provision of 400 scholarships for a period of five years for training Ghanaian specialists in various scientific and technical fields, which is covered under Article 6 of the Cultural Co-operation Agreement. The German Democratic Republic side stated they could not conveniently accommodate 400 students annually. They agreed, however, to offer scholarships for 30 Ghanaian students for higher studies during the academic year 1962/63, detailed arrangements of which will have to be worked out later by representatives of the two Governments. They pointed out that there are already 25 Ghanaian scholarship students in the German Democratic Republic.

(Krobo Edusei)
LEADER, GHANA TRADE AND ECONOMIC DELEGATION.

1st November, 1961.

Abkommen zwischen der Regierung von Ghana und der Regierung der Deutschen Demokratischen Republik, 1. November 1961

STRICTLY CONFIDENTIAL

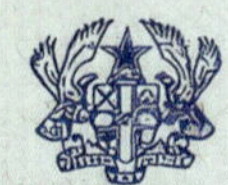

Report on Agreements signed with the Government of the Polish People's Republic

1. Terms of Reference:

The terms of reference of the Delegation are to negotiate and conclude Trade and Economic Agreements based on the Aide Memoire presented by Osagyefo Dr. Kwame Nkrumah to His Excellency Mr. Josef Cyrankiewies, Prime Minister of the Polish People's Republic during his visit to Poland in July 1961.

2. Agreements concluded:

The following Agreements (copies attached) were signed on the 26th of October, 1961 :-

(a) Long-Term Trade Agreement
(b) Long-Term Payments Agreement
(c) Addendum to the Credit Agreement signed on 19th July, 1961.

3. Summary of salient points in the Agreements:

(a) Long-Term Trade Agreement – During the discussions held in the Ministry of Foreign Trade under the chairmanship of Mr. J.Burakiewiez the Deputy Minister of Foreign Trade and Leader of the Polish delegation, it was agreed that for further expansion in the volume of Trade between the two countries, a turnover figure of £2.5-million on each side should be aimed at in the first year, rising to £5-million on each side by the end of the fifth year.

With particular reference to Cocoa, the Polish side indicated that they would be prepared to purchase 4,000 tons of cocoa beans in 1962 on condition that Ghana in turn imported 150,000 tons of cement from Poland during the same period. This was agrred upon.

It was further agreed that purchases of the above-mentioned commodities to be made by either side in subsequent years during the validity of this Agreement shall be determined by annual Protocols.

/AVTM

Agreements between the Government of Ghana and the Government of the Polish People's Republic, November 1, 1961

2.

It was further agreed that for the period fixed for the conclusion of the contracts under the previous Agreements should be extended from 30th June, 1962 to 31st December, 1962.

Regarding the other commodities to be exchanged, the following indications of requirements were also agreed upon :-

i) Commodities from Ghana:

Ground-nuts	..	5,000 tons (approx.)	per annum
Palm Kernels	..	5,000-10,000 tons	" "
Cotton	..	5,000 tons	" "
Rubber	..	2,000 "	" "

ii) Commodities from Poland:

Sugar	..	20,000 tons (approx.)	per annum
Cotton Fabrics	..	4 million Yards "	" "
Galvanised and Enamel wares	..	£250,000 (approx.)	" "

(b) Long-Term Payments Agreement - A Long-Term Payments Agreement was concluded providing a swing credit of £G500,000 free of any charges and interest.

By an addendum to the Economic Agreement which provides for repayment of the credit through the Long-Term Payments Agreement, all payments shall now be settled through the clearing account under the Long-Term Agreement.

(c) Credit Facilities - By an exchange of letters dated 20th October, 1961, the Government of the Polish People's Republic have agreed to grant a further credit of £G5-million at an interest rate of 2½ % per annum, the utilisation of which will become effective after the previous credit has been fully utilised.

It was further agreed that the period fixed for the conclusion of the contract under the previous Agreements should be extended from

30th ...../3

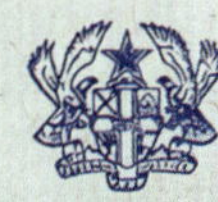

3.

30th June, 1962 to 31st December, 1962.

The Polish Government have particularly requested that a Joint Committee of representatives of both countries should meet in Accra not later than 31st December, 1961 to work out plans for the full utilisation of the previous credit of £G5-million and submit its report to both Governments not later than 31st January, 1962.

(d) Training Facilities - With reference to paragraph 5 of the Aide Memoire regarding the request for specialist training facilities for 500 Ghanaian students annually, the Polish side were not in a position to make any specific offers and they suggested that this matter be dealt with by the Joint Committee to be set up in accordance with the provisions of Article 7 of the Agreement on Scientific and Technical Co-operation concluded on the 19th April, 1961.

(Krobo Edusei)
LEADER, GHANA TRADE AND ECONOMIC DELEGATION

1st November, 1961.

Abkommen zwischen der Regierung von Ghana und der Regierung der Volksrepublik Polen, 1. November 1961

funding from the World Bank and other international sources. Completed in 1965, the dam was one of Nkrumah's most ambitious projects. It resulted in the creation of Lake Volta, the world's largest artificial lake at the time, and generated hydroelectric power designed to support industrialization efforts, including the operation of the Volta Aluminum Company (VALCO) smelter. The dam played a crucial role in boosting electricity generation, which was essential for advancing Ghana's process of industrialization.

Although Tema Harbor was primarily funded by the Ghanaian government, it benefited from international technical assistance during its construction. The project was managed by the construction contractors Sir William Halcrow and Partners Ltd. Operational since 1962, Tema Harbor transformed the city into a significant industrial hub. Designed as a planned city with dedicated industrial zones, the port greatly facilitated Ghana's trade, cocoa exports in particular. It

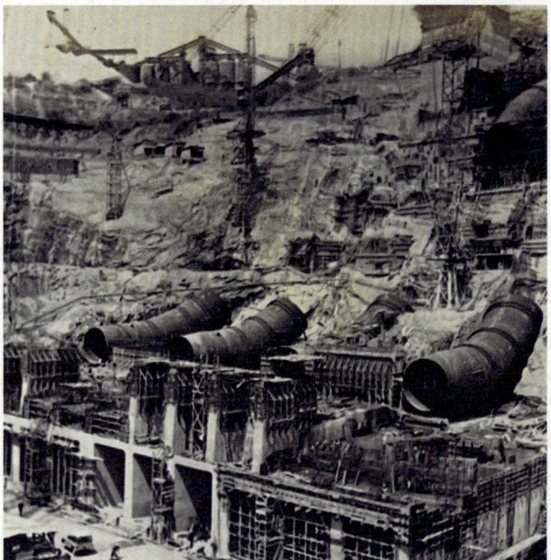

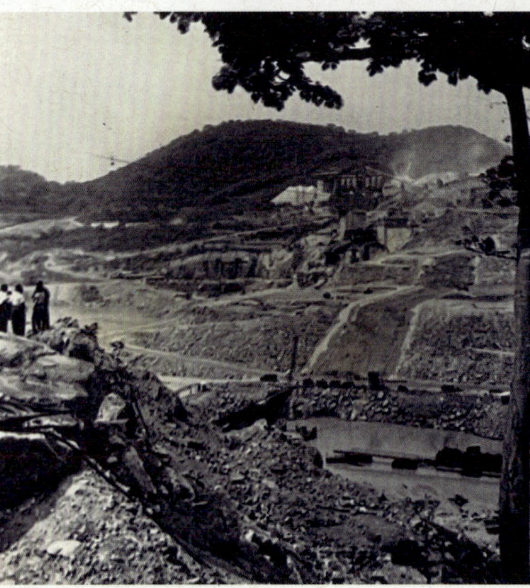

Photos of the building of the Akosombo Dam (1961–1965), which was constructed by an Italian consortium, Impregilo

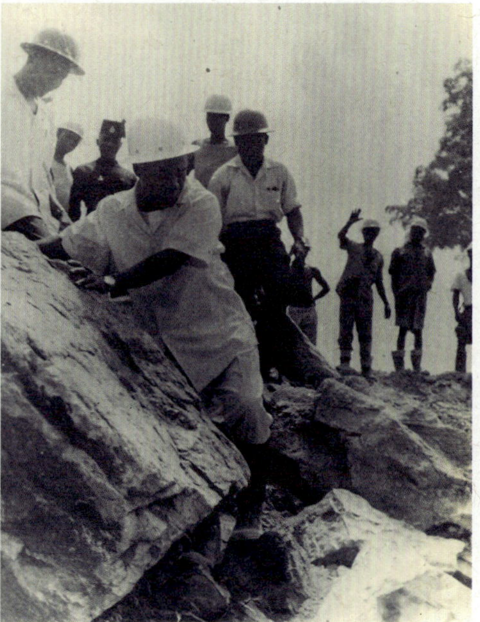

Fotos vom Bau des Akosombo-Staudamms (1961–1965), der von dem italienischen Konsortium Impregilo errichtet wurde

„Wir blicken nicht nach Osten und nicht nach Westen: Wir blicken nach vorn.“[6]

Diese strategischen Allianzen, Kollaborationen und Partnerschaften halfen dabei, einige bedeutende Industrie- und Infrastrukturprojekte in Ghana zu lancieren. Zu den wichtigsten Resultaten dieser Partnerschaften zählen:

Der Akosombo-Staudamm als Teil des Volta-Fluss-Projekts. Er wurde in Zusammenarbeit mit der US-Firma Kaiser Aluminium gebaut und erhielt erhebliche Fördermittel von der Weltbank und aus anderen internationalen Finanzquellen. 1965 fertiggestellt, war der Staudamm eines von Nkrumahs ambitioniertesten Projekten. Durch diesen entstand der Volta-Stausee, zur damaligen Zeit der größte künstliche See weltweit, und er lieferte mit seinem Wasserkraftwerk Elektrizität, um die Industrialisierungsbemühungen zu unterstützen, darunter den Betrieb der Aluminiumhütte Volta Aluminium Company (VALCO). Der Staudamm spielte eine wesentliche Rolle beim Ankurbeln der Stromerzeugung, die

6. *Selected Speeches: Kwame Nkrumah*, hg. von Samuel Obeng, Bd. 1, Accra: Afram Publications 1979, S. 52.

bolstered Ghana's mercantile capabilities and aligned with Nkrumah's vision of a robust industrial base, whose establishment would lead to the growth of Tema as one of the country's key industrial centers.

The Ghana Atomic Energy Commission (GAEC) was established in 1963 with support from both the Soviet Union and the United States through the "Atoms for Peace" program. Driven by Nkrumah's vision for scientific and technological advancement, GAEC was created to lead the country's efforts in nuclear energy development. While the anticipated progress in nuclear power did not fully materialize, GAEC's establishment was pivotal in laying the foundation for scientific research in nuclear science and technology in Ghana.

Ghana's industrial estates received technical and financial support from the Soviet Union, China, and Yugoslavia. Nkrumah's government established these estates in Accra, Tema, and other locations to accommodate industries such as textiles, food processing, and manufacturing. This initiative was part of Nkrumah's broader strategy of diversifying the economy and lessening reliance on agricultural exports like cocoa. Despite the ambitious goals, many of these industries faced difficulties owing to poor management, a shortage of skilled labor, and financial challenges.

The Tema Printing Press was constructed between 1962 and 1964 through a partnership between Polygraph Export Limited and the Ghana National Construction Corporation (GNCC, Construction Department). Essential machinery and technical expertise were provided by the German Democratic Republic (East Germany). This assistance from Eastern Bloc countries was part of their broader Cold War strategy to support newly independent nations and was deeply influenced by socialist ideologies.

HARLEM
by Langston Hughes

What happens to a dream deferred?
Does it dry up

für das Voranschreiten der Industrialisierung in Ghana von entscheidender Bedeutung war.

Auch wenn der Bau des Seehafens Tema vorwiegend von der ghanaischen Regierung finanziert wurde, profitierte das Vorhaben von internationaler technischer Unterstützung. Das Projekt wurde geleitet vom Bauunternehmen Sir William Halcrow and Partners Ltd. Seit 1962 in Betrieb, hat der Hafen von Tema die Stadt in ein bedeutendes Industriezentrum verwandelt. Entworfen als Planstadt mit ausgewiesenen Industriegebieten, brachte die Hafenanlage dem Land enorme Erleichterungen beim Handel, insbesondere bei den Kakao-Exporten. Sie stärkte das Leistungsvermögen des ghanaischen Handelssektors, fügte sich in Nkrumahs Vision der Etablierung einer stabilen Wirtschaftsbasis und führte dazu, dass Tema zu einem der führenden Industriezentren des Landes heranwuchs.

Die Ghana Atomic Energy Commission (GAEC) wurde 1963 mit Unterstützung der Sowjetunion wie der Vereinigten Staaten im Rahmen des Programms „Atomkraft für den Frieden“ gegründet. Angetrieben von Nkrumahs Vision des wissenschaftlichen und technologischen Fortschritts wurde die ghanaische Atomenergiekommission GAEC gegründet, um bei den Bemühungen des Landes um die Entwicklung der Kernenergie die Führungsrolle zu übernehmen. Auch wenn sich die erwarteten Fortschritte bei der Kernenergie nicht in vollem Umfang einstellten, war die Gründung der GAEC doch von entscheidender Bedeutung, um die wissenschaftliche Forschung im Bereich der nuklearen Wissenschaften und Technologien in Ghana auf ein solides Fundament zu stellen.

Die ghanaischen Industrieparks erhielten technische und finanzielle Unterstützung von der Sowjetunion, China und Jugoslawien. Nkrumahs Regierung errichtete diese Parks in Accra, Tema und an anderen Orten, um dort die Textilindustrie, die Lebensmittelverarbeitung und das verarbeitende Gewerbe anzusiedeln. Diese Initiative war Teil von Nkrumahs umfassenderer Strategie zur Diversifizierung der Wirtschaft und zur Verringerung der Abhängigkeit von Agrarexporten wie dem Kakao. Trotz der ehrgeizigen Ziele hatten viele dieser Betriebe mit Schwierigkeiten zu kämpfen, die auf schlechtes Management, einen Mangel an qualifizierten Arbeitskräften und finanzielle Probleme zurückzuführen waren.

Die Tema Printing Press wurde zwischen 1962 und 1964 im Rahmen einer Partnerschaft zwischen der Polygraph Export GmbH und der Ghana National

TEMA PRESS, PHYSICAL PROOF OF GHANA'S INDUSTRIALISATION

Yesterday, Osagyefo Dr. Kwame Nkrumah, unveiled a plaque to declare open, the Tema Printing Press.

And below is the full text of the speech delivered by Mr. A. E. Inkumsah, Minister of Information and Broadcasting during the occasion:

THERE are moments in the life of a nation that mark the end of one era and the beginning of another. Epoch-making events which although may not be realised at the time, are of the greatest significance in the forward march of a people.

One such event is this afternoon's ceremony to mark the formal opening of this magnificent Printing Press by no less an august person than our beloved and most revered and illustrious leader, Dr. Kwame Nkrumah. It therefore gives me the greatest pleasure to have this opportunity of addressing you on this occasion.

Friendship

I would like first of all to welcome on behalf of the Ministry, our friends from the German Democratic Republic, especially the Deputy Prime Minister, His Excellency, Mr. Paul Scholz, whose presence here with us at this historic function emphasises the significance of the ever-growing bonds of friendship between the two countries.

This magnificent Printing Press, as you can see for yourselves, is only one of the many projects symbolising the resurgent spirit of our national reconstruction. Like several other projects and industries being tackled in earnest all over the country, it is a physical proof of the high tempo of the planned industrialisation of this country, and evidence of the sense of urgency with which we are determined to implement the Seven-Year Development Plan, the brainchild of our beloved Leader.

This Printing Press is also a perfect example of what can be achieved through hard work and collaboration between the Ghana Government and friendly countries genuinely interested in helping us to achieve the objectives of the socialist path of economic development which, under the wise, able and dynamic leadership of Osagyefo, we have chosen for ourselves. I refer in this instance to the German Democratic Republic who have played an important role in the establishment of this Printing Press.

Careful Study

The decision to establish a Printing Press of this magnitude and with it a National Publishing House was taken after a most careful appraisal of the printing requirements of this country, and in relation to the educational programme which the Government has mapped out for this country.

The fast pace of development in all aspects of our national life since Independence created a large and growing demand for printed material of all kinds from institutions of learning, Government Departments and commercial establishments.

Our disabilities in the field of printing were, in 1951, accentuated by the decision of the Government to supply free text-books to all schools through the country at a cost estimated at £G3½ million during the first year of the Plan.

It was one of the features of the colonial economy bequeathed to us that the printing capacity of the then existing presses in both Government and the private sectors of the economy was grossly inadequate to cope with the ever-growing printing needs that follow naturally in the wake of accelerated economic expansion.

Great Pressure

In spite of the new Assembly Press which was built in 1952 soon after the Convention People's Party came into power, the pressure on the Government Printing Department was so great that that Department was constantly giving out work on contract to private printers.

In even more advanced forms of printing and colour work, these had to be undertaken abroad at great loss of time and expense. In these circumstances, it was clear the Government had to do something urgent if the growing printing requirements of the country were to be adequately met and if the increasing importation of the printed matter was to be quickly arrested and progressively reduced.

I am glad to say that the Tema Press, being the direct result of the Government's quick and timely action has, as in the case of several other projects initiated by the Government, proved the wisdom of the forward-looking policies of the Government and vindicated once more the rationality of socialist pattern of economy which we are rapidly evolving to suit our own African conditions.

Satisfaction

Education is the corner-stone of progress in every society and printing and publishing are the most powerful vehicles for accelerated education. It is therefore a matter of deep satisfaction to me that within the comparatively short space of three years when my Ministry concluded negotiations with Messrs. Polygraph Export G.M.B.H. of Berlin, who are world-famous suppliers of printing machinery, for the establishment of a modern press at Tema, we have today completed these magnificent buildings which are equipped with some of the most modern and up-to-date printing machinery comparable in quality to any that may be found anywhere in the world.

Ladies and Gentlemen, with the establishment of this Tema Printing Press, we have travelled a long way from 1857 when the then Colonial Government signed an order at Cape Coast Castle for a printing machine from the United Kingdom.

Those were the days of bureaucratic procedure and slow-moving administration, and it took no less than 17 years between the signing of the order and the actual installation of the equipment — a simple letter press machine which was hand-operated by a staff of seven

It was not until 1902 when the first Government Printer was appointed. By 1907 the first Monotype apparatus had been installed and for the first time, type casting began at the Press.

This machine, which was operated by two men, had a capacity of producing seven times the amount of set matter that could be produced by a hand compositor. The next milestone was reached in 1930 with the installation of Linotype Machines to accelerate the execution of jobs and remove, once and for all, the setting of matter by hand.

Twenty further years were still to elapse before one Timson Rotary Printing Press was installed and this especially designed to print receipt books and general counterfoil receipts.

I have recapitulated these few land-marks in the history of Printing in this country to enable you to appreciate the rapid progress which we have made in all areas of Government activity since the Convention People's Party, under the inspired leadership of Osagyefo Dr. Kwame Nkrumah, came into power.

Mechanised One

Unlike existing presses in the country today, the Tema Printing Press is mechanised and has very modern automatic machines designed to ensure speed, uniformity and economy in production.

Set in these splendid surroundings, the buildings consist office Production Halls, a four-storey Administration block, one of which will accommodate the National Publishing House and Editorial offices and also a large Dining Hall and Kitchen which can cater for 250 persons in one shift and Dressing Rooms which are equipped with hot and cold running water. I am pleased to say that the best provision has been made to cater for the comfort and happiness of the workers in this Printing Press.

The Production Halls are themselvss built in such a way as to ensure an even flow of production through the various stages of printing, hand composing, intertype, monotype and chemigraphy

Hall Two is for the rotary, flat presses and the manufac-

* (Trun to Page 5)

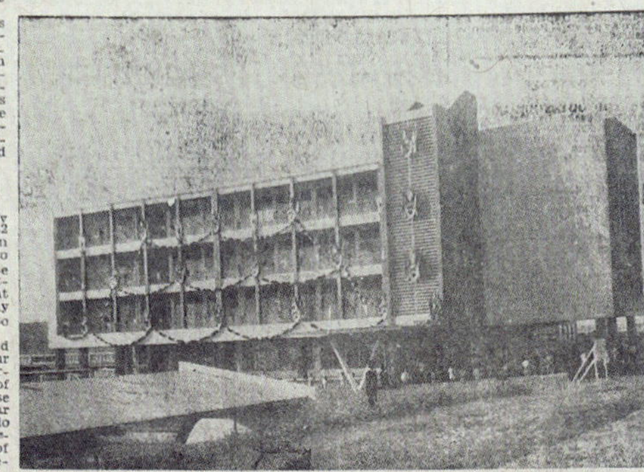

This is the front view of the magnificent Tema Printing Press.

Newspaper clipping, *Evening News*, September 26, 1964, p. 3. "Tema Press, Physical Proof of Ghana's Industrialisation"

Zeitungsausschnitte, *Evening News*, 26. September 1964, S. 3: „Tema Press, Physical Proof of Ghana's Industrialisation"

EVENING NEWS, SATURDAY, SEPTEMBER 26, 1964 Page 5

TEMA PRESS WILL EMPLOY 600 STRONG LABOUR FORCE

OSAGYEFO INSPECTS A MACHINE

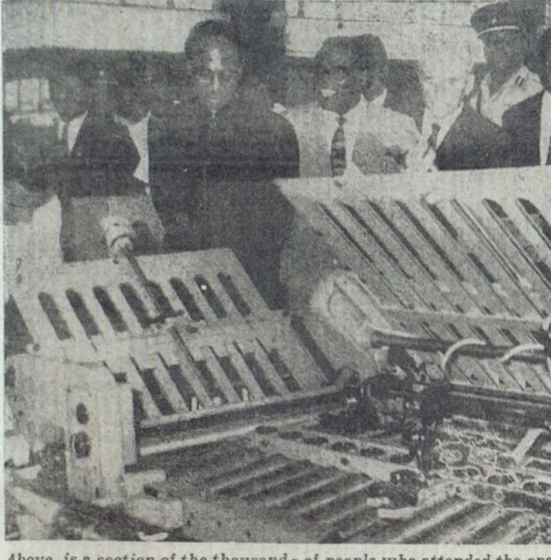

Above, is a section of the thousands of people who attended the opening ceremony of the press at Tema yesterday.

G. D. R. plays an important role

★ (Continued from Page 3)

ture of copy books. The Third Hall is exclusively for offset printing; the Fourth Hall for book-binding, and the Fifth Hall for papers for the whole Printing Press.

With its most modern equipment which is 60 per cent offset and 40 per cent letter press, this Printing Press will be able to undertake all forms of printing from newspaper production to highly skilled, artistic and literary publications of a wide range.

I need hardly say therefore that the establishment of this Press opens out a long vista of opportunities for our printing and publishing potential. A wave of cultural revivalism is today sweeping relentlessly across the continent of Africa.

Optimum Use

Our resurgent desire to recapture the glory of our culture and to blend with the best that is available in this age of highly advanced technology and sophisticated civilisation makes it imperative that we make optimum use of this Press.

I feel sure that with the establishment of this Press, the literary and cultural currents in the African revolution will gather momentum, and speed up the dissemination of knowledge so essestial in the movement for a continental Union Government for Africa.

I am informed that when this Press is running at full capacity it will employ a labour force of some 600 workers in two shifts of 300 persons each. I have every confidence that every worker in this Printing Press whatever his job may be, will put into it the energy, enthusiasm and pride that goes into the creation of all great ventures into which so much public money has been sunk.

Success

Upon the results of their collective efforts and the success that they make of their jobs, rests the future of this Printing Press.

At this stage, I would like to express my appreciation for the efforts that have gone into the erection of these buildings and the machines.

I thank especially Messrs Bushman and Hoehne and the rest of the Polygraph Consultants and Engineers, who have been responsible for the supervision of this project; the Ghana National Construction Corporation for the high degree of workmanship which is evident in the construction of these buildings and last but not the least the officials of my Ministry who have co-ordinated the administrative arrangements for the execution of this project.

Distinguished Guests, Ladies and Gentlemen it is gratifying to witness today yet another milestone in the rapid industrial development of our country. It is my hope that this Press will turn out publications that will not only enlighten our people but also speed up our march towards our goal of one Continental Government.

And now, Ladies and Gentlemen I have the greatest pleasure, respectfully to invite Osagyefo our illustrious Philosopher and President Father of our dynamic nation, and our constant guiding light to unveil the plaque to mark the formal opening of the Tema Printing Press.

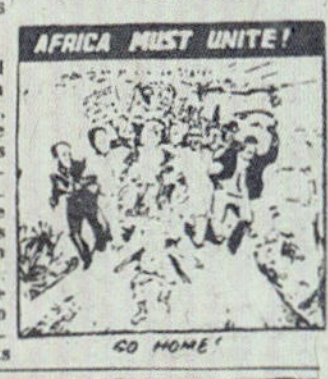

...AND THE PEOPLE WERE THERE IN THEIR THOUSANDS

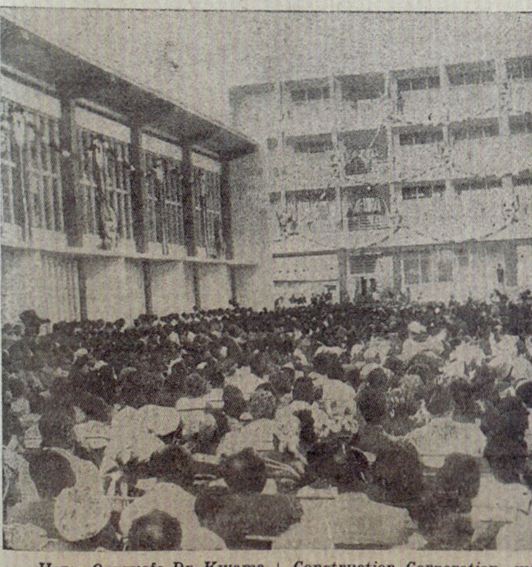

Here, Osagyefo Dr Kwame Nkrumah inspects one of the numerous machines at the press which has been described as the most modern and equipped printing press in West Africa.

The press which was constructed by the Ghana National Construction Corporation, will employ 600 workers.

The engineering work on the press was supervised by Messrs Bushman and Hoehne of the German Democratic Republic Polygraph Consultants and Engineers.

Newspaper clipping, *Evening News*, September 26, 1964.
Left: Kwame Nkrumah at the opening of the Tema Printing Press. Right: Members of the public at the opening of the Tema Printing Press

Zeitungsausschnitte, *Evening News*, 26. September 1964, links: Kwame Nkrumah bei der Eröffnung der Tema Printing Press, rechts: Bürger·innen bei der Eröffnung der Tema Printing Press

like a raisin in the sun?
Or fester like a sore—
And then run?
Does it stink like rotten meat?
Or crust and sugar over—
like a syrupy sweet?

Maybe it just sags
like a heavy load.

Or does it explode?[7]

The *beautyful* ones that were never born . . .[8]

Imagine, if you will, a nation standing on the brink of its own destiny, only for it to be thwarted by the conniving hands of detractors, both at home and abroad. Despite his grand vision and relentless efforts to modernize Ghana, Nkrumah's leadership was eventually cut short. On February 24, 1966, while he was on a diplomatic mission to Vietnam and China, his government was overthrown in a military coup orchestrated by the National Liberation Council. The coup was not just a domestic affair; there is substantial evidence suggesting Western involvement, particularly on the part of the Central Intelligence Agency (CIA), which saw Nkrumah's socialist policies and alignment with the Eastern Bloc as a threat to Western interests during the Cold War. The nightmarish part of his dream that was always lurking in the shadows took over.

The years that followed the overthrow of Nkrumah marked a significant retrogression for Ghana's ambitious development agenda. Many of the industrial projects and infrastructure initiatives that were in progress or had been completed under his administration were either halted or neglected. The new military government adopted a more conservative economic approach, which often meant dismantling Nkrumah's socialist policies and undoing the strategic alliances he had

7. Langston Hughes, "Harlem," in *Selected Poems of Langston Hughes* (Vintage Books, 1990), 268.

8. Borrowing from Ayi Kwei Armah's intentional [mis]spelling of "beautiful" in the title of his 1968 book *The Beautyful Ones Are Not Yet Born.*

Construction Corporation (GNCC, Bauabteilung) errichtet. Wesentliche Maschinen und technisches Fachwissen wurden von der Deutschen Demokratischen Republik bereitgestellt. Diese von Ländern des Ostblocks gewährten Hilfen fügten sich in ihre allgemeine Strategie während des Kalten Krieges ein, die neuen unabhängig gewordenen Nationen zu unterstützen, und sie waren stark von sozialistischen Ideologien geprägt.

HARLEM
von Langston Hughes

What happens to a dream deferred?
Does it dry up
like a raisin in the sun?
Or fester like a sore –
And then run?
Does it stink like rotten meat?
Or crust and sugar over –
like a syrupy sweet?

Maybe it just sags
like a heavy load.

Or does it explode?[7]

Die Schönen, die nie geboren wurden …[8]

Stellen Sie sich eine Nation vor, die an der Schwelle steht, ihr Schicksal in die eigene Hand zu nehmen, nur um diese Bestrebungen dann von hinterhältigen Gegnern im In- und Ausland vereitelt zu sehen. Trotz seiner großen Vision und seines unermüdlichen Einsatzes für die Modernisierung Ghanas fand Nkrumahs Führung schließlich ein vorzeitiges, abruptes Ende. Am 24. Februar 1966, als Nkrumah sich auf einer diplomatischen Mission in Vietnam und China befand, wurde seine Regierung durch einen vom Nationalen Befreiungsrat orchestrierten Militärputsch

7. Langston Hughes, „Harlem", in: *Selected Poems of Langston Hughes*, New York: Vintage Books 1990, S. 268.

8. Im Original: „The beautyful ones that were never born ..." In Anlehnung an Ayi Kwei Armahs bewusste (Falsch-)Schreibung von „beautiful" im Titel seines 1968 erschienen Buchs *The Beautyful Ones Are Not Yet Born.*

cultivated. This shift not only slowed down Ghana's industrialization process but also led to a broader decline in the country's economic and social development.

So, we're left to ask: What might have been? How different could the future of Ghana—and Africa as a whole—have looked if Nkrumah's vision had been allowed to fully develop? These questions linger, not as an attempt to romanticize the past but as a means of examining pivotal moments to better understand the present and forge new future(s). Hopefully, we can avoid the haunting echoes of "the beautyful ones that were never born," those lost possibilities and unfulfilled dreams that might have (re)shaped a nation and a continent.

Editor's note: This version of *Amidst the Ambivalent Promises, the Roses Faded and the Dreams Disappeared* was first given as a presentation by the author on September 28, 2021, at the DECOSO Meeting #3, titled "Reflexive Tema and Global Elsewheres . . ."

gestürzt. Der Staatsstreich war nicht nur eine innenpolitische Angelegenheit; es gibt zahlreiche Hinweise auf eine Beteiligung des Westens, insbesondere der Central Intelligence Agency (CIA), die in Nkrumahs sozialistischer Politik und seiner Annäherung an den Ostblock eine Bedrohung für die westlichen Interessen während des Kalten Krieges sah. Der alptraumhafte Teil seines Traums, der immer im Verborgenen lauerte, drängte sich nun in den Vordergrund.

Die auf den Sturz Nkrumahs folgenden Jahre markierten einen erheblichen Rückschritt für Ghanas ambitionierte Entwicklungsagenda. Viele der unter seiner Regierung begonnenen oder fertiggestellten Industrieprojekte und Infrastrukturinitiativen wurden entweder eingestellt oder vernachlässigt. Die neue Militärregierung verfolgte einen konservativeren wirtschaftlichen Ansatz, was in vielen Fällen die Rücknahme von Nkrumahs sozialistischer Politik bedeutete sowie den Abbruch der von ihm kultivierten strategischen Allianzen. Dieser Politikwechsel führte nicht nur zu einer Verlangsamung von Ghanas Industrialisierungsprozess, sondern auch zu einem großflächigen Niedergang der wirtschaftlichen und gesellschaftlichen Entwicklung des Landes insgesamt.

Es bleibt uns also zu fragen: Was hätte sein können? Wie anders könnte die Zukunft Ghanas – und Afrikas als Ganzem – ausgesehen haben, wenn sich Nkrumahs Vision vollständig hätte entfalten können? Diese Fragen bleiben bestehen, nicht als Versuch, die Vergangenheit zu romantisieren, sondern als ein Ansatz zur Untersuchung von historischen Schlüsselmomenten, um ein besseres Verständnis der Gegenwart zu erlangen und eine neue Zukunft oder neue Zukünfte zu schmieden. Hoffentlich können wir die quälenden Echos „der Schönen, die nie geboren wurden" vermeiden, diese verlorenen Gelegenheiten und unerfüllten Träume, die vielleicht eine Nation und einen Kontinent (um)gestaltet hätten.

Anmerkung der Herausgeberin: Diese Version von *Unter den zwiespältigen Versprechungen verwelkten die Rosen und verschwanden die Träume* wurde vom Autor zuerst präsentiert am 28. September 2021 auf dem DECOSO Meeting #3, mit dem Titel „Reflexive Tema and Global Elsewheres".

FRAGMENTS OF NATIONHOOD (2024)

Ato Annan

FRAGMENTE NATIONALER IDENTITAT (2024)

Fragments of Nationhood explores the complex and contested legacy of Kwame Nkrumah's symbolic nationalism, focusing on his deliberate crafting of Ghanaian identity through the manipulation of national symbols, particularly his decision to have his image minted on the country's new currency in the period immediately following independence. During his tenure as Ghana's first leader from 1957 until his overthrow in 1966, Nkrumah positioned himself as the embodiment of the new Ghanaian state. How did this impact the nation's identity? In what ways were his image and persona intertwined with the nation's fabric?

Fragments of Nationhood reflects on Nkrumah's unprecedented efforts to stamp his identity on the country's consciousness. Through the minting of coins, the issuance of stamps, the creation of monuments in his likeness, and the redesign of national symbols such as the anthem and flag, Nkrumah sought to cement himself as the "Founder of the State of Ghana." What does this say about the nature of leadership and legacy when personal identity is so deeply enmeshed with national symbols? After his ousting in 1966, many of these icons were dismantled or reinterpreted, as successive governments sought to reshape Ghana's historical narrative, debating the extent of Nkrumah's legacy and influence. To what extent did the dismantling of his legacy alter our understanding of nationhood?

This body of work draws on this complex history, using archival photos, text, and documents—mainly from the Münzkabinett (Coin Cabinet) of the Staatliche Kunstsammlungen Dresden (Dresden State Art Collections, SKD), the National Archives of Ghana, the Photo Department of the Information Services Department of Ghana, various archives, and online sources—to create collages that deconstruct and reassemble these national symbols, illustrating the fluidity of political memory and the fragile nature of nationhood. These collages underscore how Nkrumah's once immovable image was contested, demonized, debated, and, in many cases, re-engineered to align with new political realities. This is an invitation to reflect on the power of national symbols in shaping collective identity and on how history is an ever-evolving construct molded by those in power. It also serves as both a tribute and a critical examination of Nkrumah's place in Ghanaian history and as a provocation to consider how national heroes are made, remade, or erased.

Fragmente nationaler Identität (*Fragments of Nationhood*) erkundet das komplexe und umstrittene Erbe von Kwame Nkrumahs symbolischem Nationalismus und konzentriert sich dabei auf die von ihm bewusst vorgenommene Formung der ghanaischen Identität durch die Manipulation nationaler Symbole. Ein besonderes Augenmerk liegt auf seiner Entscheidung, in der unmittelbar auf die Unabhängigkeit folgenden Zeit sein Antlitz auf die Münzen der neuen Währung des Landes prägen zu lassen. Während seiner Amtszeit als Ghanas erstes Staatsoberhaupt von 1957 bis zu seinem Sturz 1966 brachte Nkrumah sich selbst als Verkörperung des neuen ghanaischen Staates in Stellung. Wie hat das die Identität der Nation beeinflusst? Auf welche Weise waren sein Erscheinungsbild und seine Persona mit dem Gefüge der Nation verflochten?

Fragmente nationaler Identität ist eine Reflexion über Nkrumahs beispiellose Versuche, dem Bewusstsein des Landes den Stempel seiner Identität aufzudrücken. Durch das Prägen von Münzen, die Ausgabe von Briefmarken, den Bau von Denkmälern mit seinem Ebenbild und durch die Neugestaltung nationaler Symbole wie der Nationalhymne und der Landesflagge trachtete Nkrumah danach, seinen Status als „Gründer des Staates Ghana" zu zementieren. Was sagt das aus über das Wesen von politischer Führung und politischem Vermächtnis, wenn die persönliche Identität so tief mit nationalen Symbolen verschlungen ist? Nach seiner Amtsenthebung 1966 wurden viele dieser Ikonen niedergerissen oder neu interpretiert, da die nachfolgenden Regierungen bestrebt waren, das historische Narrativ Ghanas umzuschreiben, und dabei das Ausmaß von Nkrumahs Vermächtnis und Einfluss zur Diskussion stellten. Inwieweit hat die Demontage seiner Hinterlassenschaften unser Verständnis von nationaler Identität verändert?

Dieses Werk schöpft aus dieser komplexen Geschichte und verwendet Fotos, Texte und Dokumente aus Archivbeständen – hauptsächlich aus dem Münzkabinett der Staatlichen Kunstsammlungen Dresden (SKD), den National Archives of Ghana, der Fotografischen Abteilung des Information Services Department of Ghana, verschiedenen weiteren Archiven und Onlinequellen –, um Collagen zu schaffen, die diese nationalen Symbole dekonstruieren und neu zusammenfügen. Sie illustrieren die Fluidität der politischen Erinnerung und den fragilen Charakter nationaler Identität. Diese Collagen unterstreichen, wie Nkrumahs einst unerschütterliches Image angefochten, dämonisiert, zur Debatte gestellt worden ist

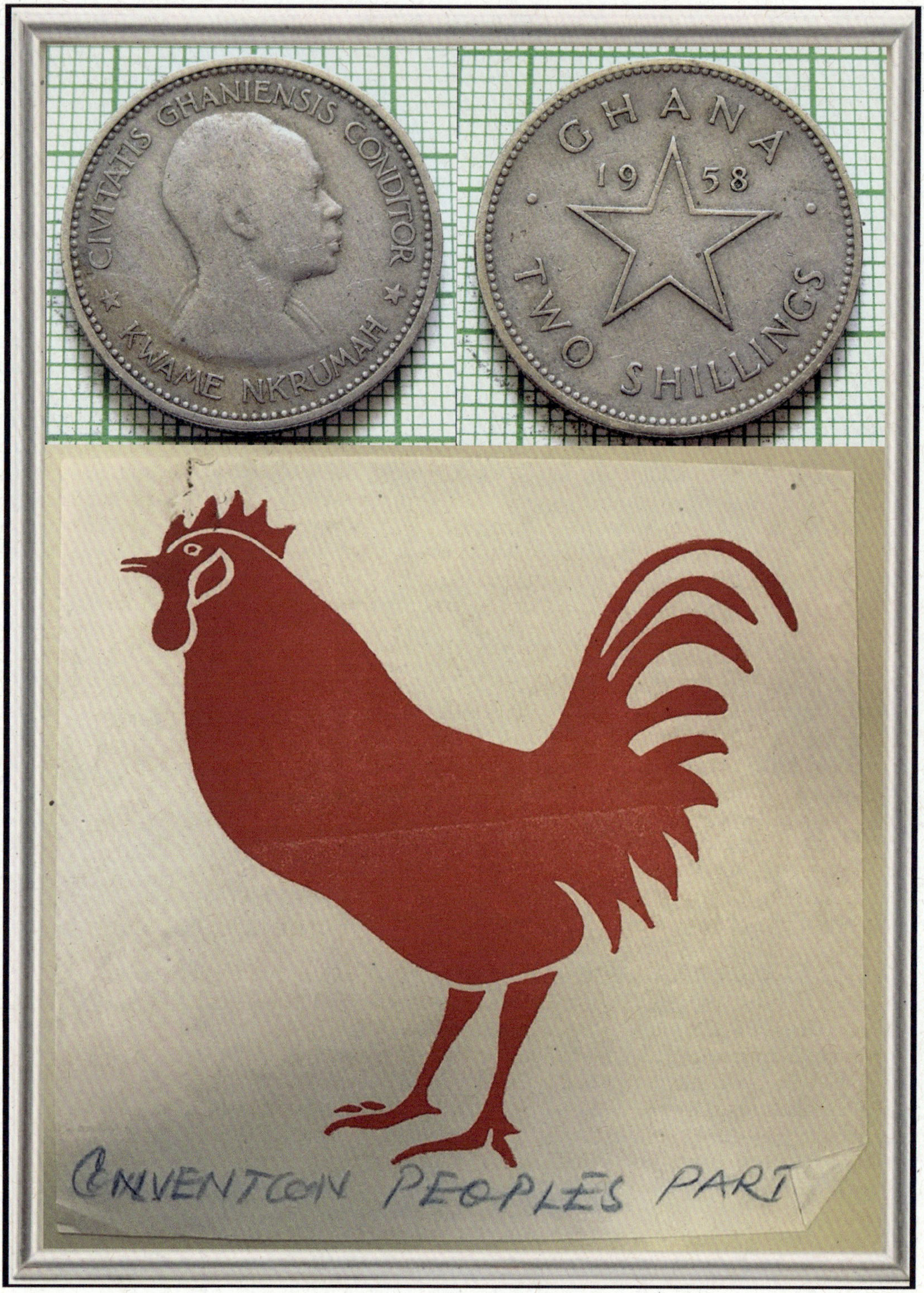

Ato Annan, *Two Shillings—Etched in Silver, Faded in Time* (1958), *Fragments of Nationhood*, 2024, digital collage, 60 cm × 45 cm

Ato Annan, *Zwei Shilling – geätzt in Silber, verwaschen in der Zeit* (1958), *Fragmente nationaler Identität*, 2024, digitale Collage, 60 cm × 45 cm

und in vielen Fällen umgearbeitet wurde, um es mit neuen politischen Realitäten zur Deckung zu bringen. Dies ist eine Einladung, über die Macht nationaler Symbole im Prozess der Herausbildung kollektiver Identität nachzudenken, und darüber, in welcher Weise Geschichte ein sich stetig weiterentwickelndes Konstrukt ist, das von denjenigen geformt wird, die an der Macht sind. Es dient darüber hinaus gleichermaßen als eine Würdigung und als eine kritische Untersuchung von Nkrumahs Platz in der Geschichte Ghanas und als eine Provokation, sich bewusst zu machen, wie Nationalhelden gemacht, umgestaltet oder ausradiert werden.

Ato Annan, *Two-Pound Coin—Golden Ashes of the Republic* (1960), *Fragments of Nationhood*, 2024, digital collage, 60 cm × 45 cm

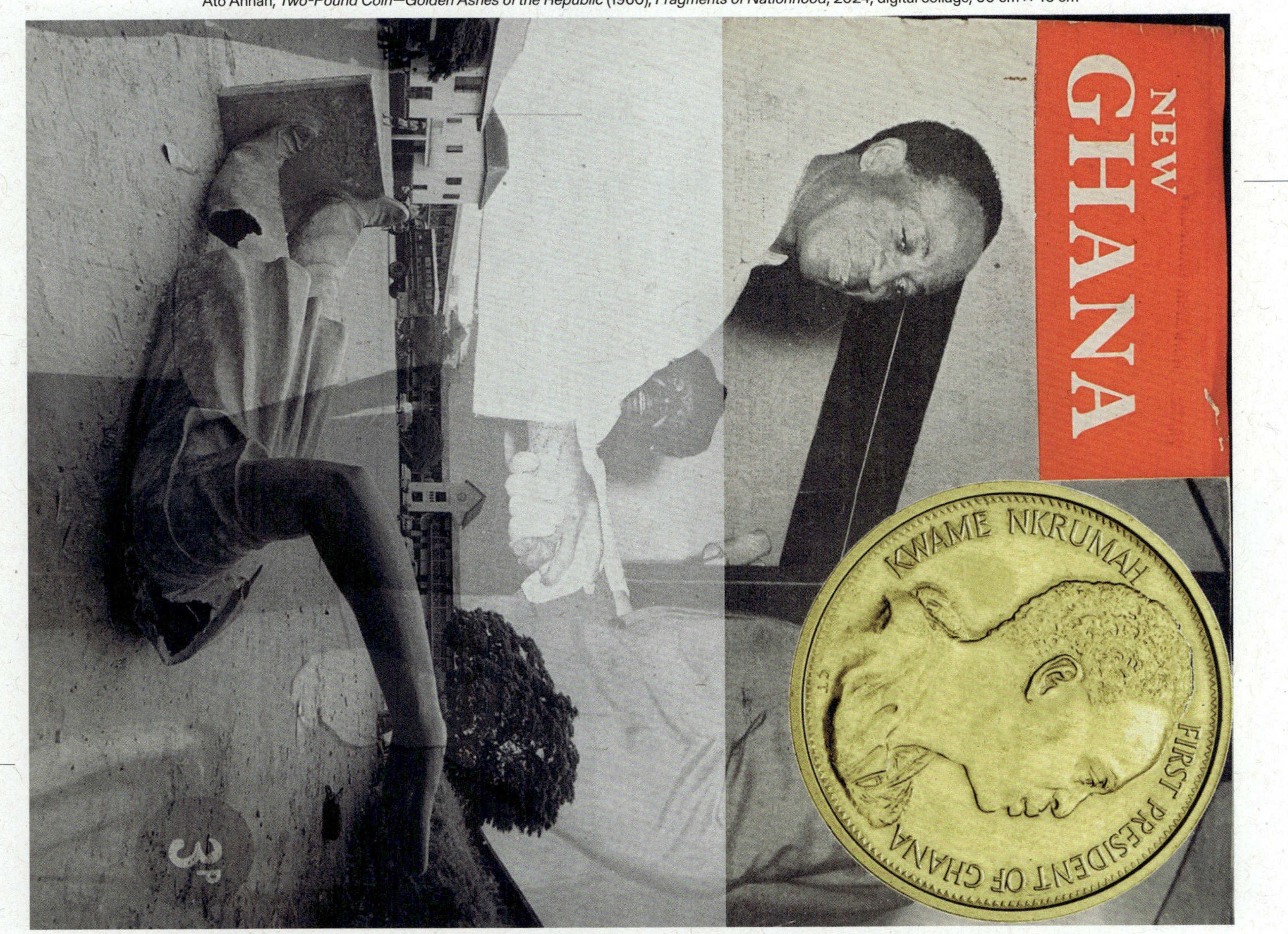

Ato Annan, *Zwei-Pfund-Münze – Goldene Asche der Republik* (1960), *Fragmente nationaler Identität*, 2024, digitale Collage, 60 cm × 45 cm

SPECIAL MESSAGE from the PRIME MINISTER to "New Nation" Readers . . .

VOTE
Dr. DANQUAH

THE long-awaited day has arrived, the day that represents the turning-point in the history of our beloved country. And we, the first proud Ghanaians, are the fortunate witnesses of this great event.

But we must not for one minute imagine that we are merely an excited and enthralled audience who have been lucky enough to secure priceless tickets for the first night of a unique performance. During the period of Independence celebrations many of us will in fact be adopting that rôle. We have worked hard and it is good and proper that we should be able to relax for a moment and reflect on the future. But this is only an interval, a mere breathing space, before we take on an even more arduous and exacting job, that of controlling and navigating our own ship of state through whatever the hazards may be that lie ahead of us.

The success of Ghana as a free, independent and sovereign state depends entirely on the individual performance of every single one among us. But the effort of each individual must be directed not for personal gain but for national reconstruction and progress. The effort must be a communal one, for if it fails we will all fall with it; if it succeeds, which it must, it will be to the grandeur and glory of our country.

UNITED EFFORT

It must be brought home to us all that the task that will face us in an independent Ghana is far, far greater than any we have had to tackle before and we will need the united effort of everyone if we are to make this country a shining example for others to follow.

We must work far harder than before and work for the good of all, with the interests of the country primarily at heart. We must work as a united body and pull together in one direction. We must be prepared for sacrifices. We must not be discouraged when our difficulties appear to get on top of us nor must we relax in self-contentment when things go well.

Remember that Ghana was not created solely for its present citizens. Our children's children and generations of Africans to come will suffer or benefit according to how we lay the foundations of this their heritage.

Let there be, as John Milton penned it—

"United thoughts and counsels, equal hope,
And hazard in the glorious enterprise."

KWAME NKRUMAH

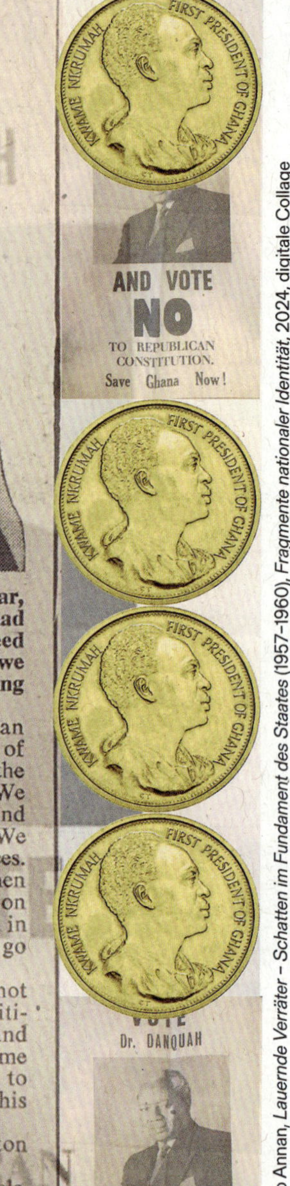

Ato Annan, *Lurking Traitors—Shadows in the State's Foundation* (1957-1960), *Fragments of Nationhood*, 2024, digital collage

Ato Annan, *Lauernde Verräter – Schatten im Fundament des Staates* (1957-1960), *Fragmente nationaler Identität*, 2024, digitale Collage

Ato Annan, *One-Penny Coin—Dust of Dreams I* (1958), *Fragments of Nationhood*, 2024, digital collage.
Image of the one-penny coin courtesy of Staatliche Kunstsammlungen Dresden (SKD), Münzkabinett

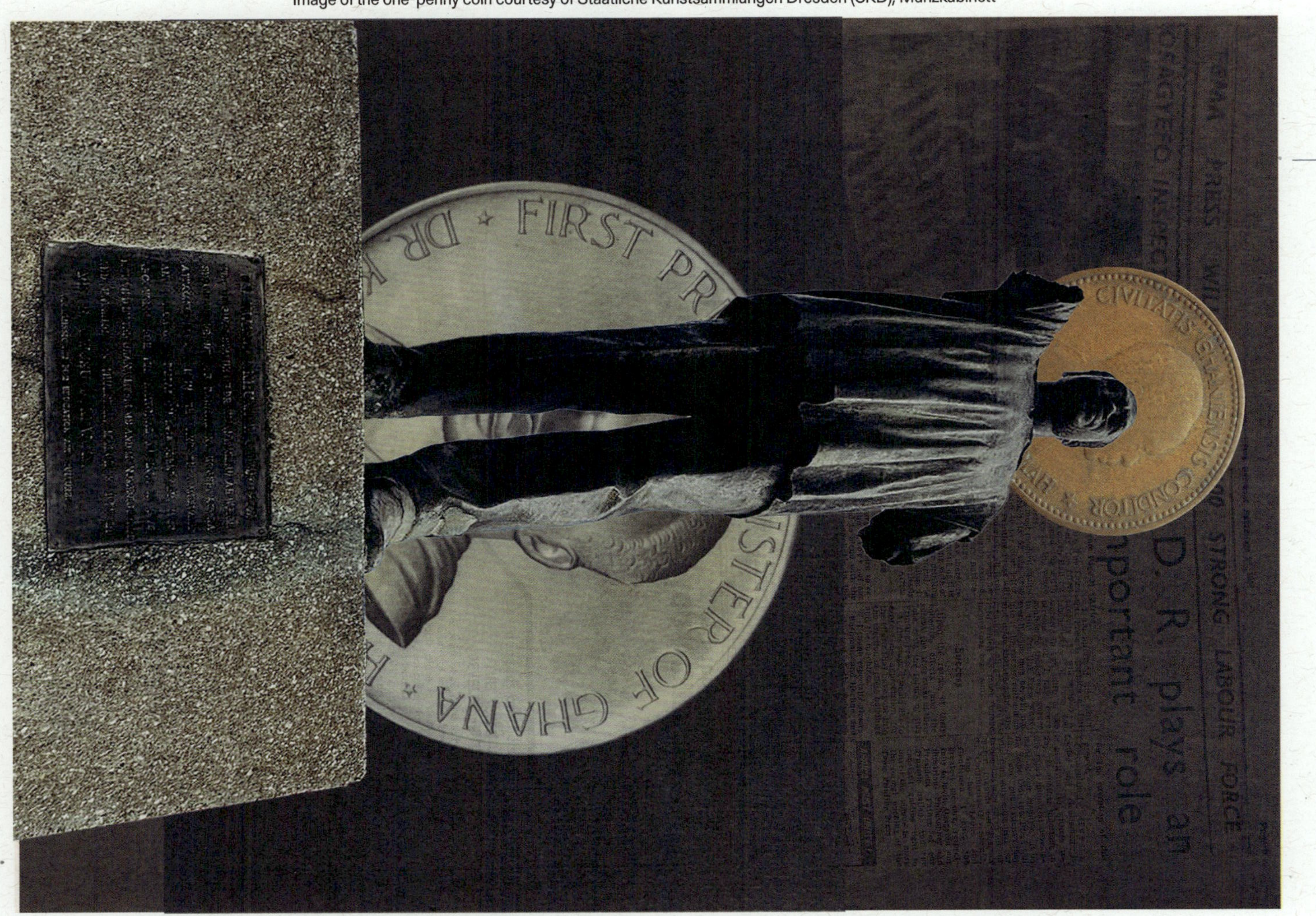

Ato Annan, *Ein Penny – Staub der Träume I* (1958), *Fragmente nationaler Identität*, 2024, digitale Collage,
Bild der Ein-Penny-Münze mit freundlicher Genehmigung der Staatlichen Kunstsammlungen Dresden (SKD), Münzkabinett

Ato Annan, *One-Penny Coin—Dust of Dreams I* (1958), *Fragments of Nationhood*, 2024, digital collage.
Image of the one-penny coin courtesy of Staatliche Kunstsammlungen Dresden (SKD), Münzkabinett

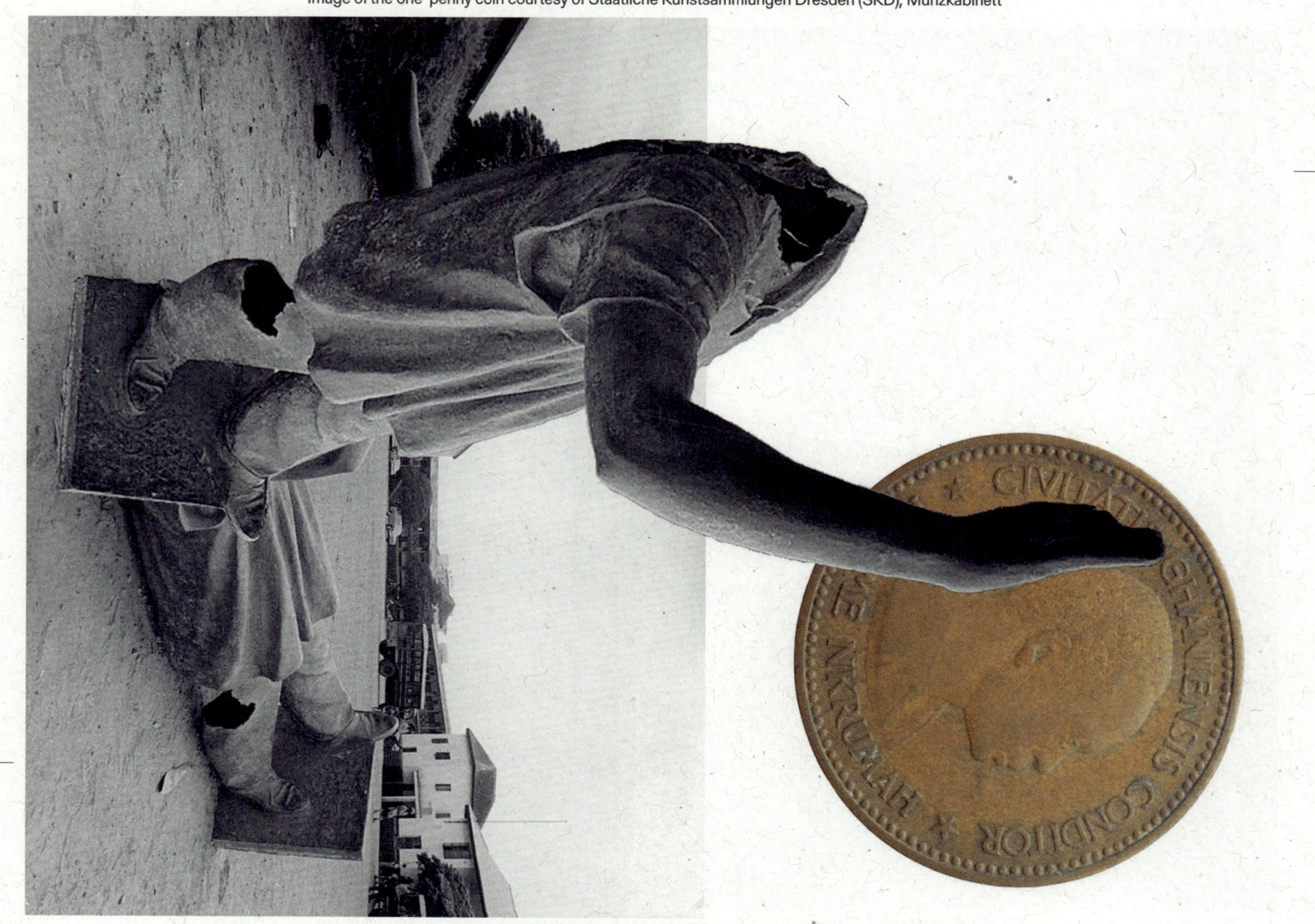

Ato Annan, *Ein Penny – Staub der Träume I* (1958), *Fragmente nationaler Identität*, 2024, digitale Collage,
Bild der Ein-Penny-Münze mit freundlicher Genehmigung der Staatlichen Kunstsammlungen Dresden (SKD), Münzkabinett

KONRAD HELBIG

GHANA, 1959

Sources:

Konrad Helbig, artist record 70055314, www.deutschefotothek.de, with extensive bibliography.

Raimund Wolfert, "Helbig, Konrad," Frankfurter Personenlexikon, August 5, 2021, https://frankfurter-personenlexikon.de/node/12345.

Thanks to Dr. Agnes Matthias of the Deutsche Fotothek for her support of this introduction.

The art historian, photojournalist, and tour guide Konrad Helbig (1917–1986) traveled to Ghana for several weeks in early 1959. Following numerous stays in the Mediterranean region, particularly in his adopted home of Marinella di Selinunte in Sicily, this journey marked Helbig's first documented visit to the African continent. The Deutsche Fotothek at the Saxon State and University Library (Sächsische Landesbibliothek – Staats- und Universitätsbibliothek, SLUB) in Dresden lists altogether 9,959 visual records by Helbig in its publicly accessible online database. Of these, 527 show portraits or document street scenes, social gatherings, and workers, along with a wide range of architectural, urban, and port views from Accra, Kumasi, Tamale, Tema, Winneba, and other locations in Ghana and from Kano in Nigeria. Almost all of them were taken in 6 × 6 cm (i.e., medium) format and in color—an unusual method at that time for photographing everyday life. The collection thus offers a unique view of the first Republic of Ghana under its president Kwame Nkrumah two years after independence. It makes visible a diversity of public places, industrial infrastructure, fashion styles, and pop cultures, as well as groups of people and individuals actively involved in shaping a postcolonial modernity. The Deutsche Fotothek acquired the Konrad Helbig estate from private ownership in 2012 and 2023. It comprises approximately 100,000 black-and-white negatives and 60,000 color slides in 6 × 6 format as well as 6,000 prints. Correspondence, lecture manuscripts, and posters are held under the signature "Mscr.Dresd.App.Helbig, Konrad" in the manuscript collection of the SLUB. Additional photographic holdings can be found in the Foto Marburg image archive (23,800 negatives), the F. C. Gundlach Foundation, and the Hamburg State Archive.

Der Kunsthistoriker, Fotopublizist und Reiseleiter Konrad Helbig (1917–1986) reiste Anfang 1959 für mehrere Wochen nach Ghana. Nach zahlreichen Aufenthalten im Mittelmeerraum, insbesondere in seiner sizilianischen Wahlheimat Marinella di Selinunte, führte ihn diese Reise erstmals auf den afrikanischen Kontinent. Die Deutsche Fotothek in Dresden verzeichnet insgesamt 9959 Bilddokumente von Helbig in ihrer öffentlich zugänglichen Online-Datenbank. 527 davon dokumentieren Straßenszenen, Zusammenkünfte, Arbeitende, außerdem finden sich Porträts sowie eine Vielzahl architektonischer, urbaner und hafennaher Ansichten aus Accra, Kumasi, Tamale, Tema, Winneba und anderen Orten in Ghana sowie aus Kano in Nigeria. Fast alle eint, dass sie in 6 × 6 cm, also im Mittelformat, und in Farbe aufgenommen wurden – in dieser Zeit eine ungewöhnliche Praxis für Alltagsfotografien. Das einzigartige Konvolut zeigt den Blick eines Reisenden auf die erste Republik von Ghana unter ihrem Präsidenten Kwame Nkrumah zwei Jahre nach Erlangung der Unabhängigkeit. Sichtbar wird eine Vielfalt von öffentlichen Orten, industrieller Infrastruktur, Fashion-Styles, Popkultur sowie Menschengruppen und Individuen, die an der Gestaltung einer postkolonialen Moderne aktiv beteiligt sind. Der Nachlass Konrad Helbig wurde 2012 und 2023 aus Privatbesitz von der Deutschen Fotothek übernommen. Er umfasst rund 100000 Schwarz-Weiß-Negative und 60000 Farbdias im Format 6 × 6 sowie 6000 Abzüge. Korrespondenzen, Vortragsmanuskripte und Plakate befinden sich unter der Signatur Mscr. Dresd. App. Helbig, Konrad in der Handschriftensammlung der Sächsischen Landesbibliothek – Staats- und Universitätsbibliothek Dresden (SLUB). Weitere Bildbestände befinden sich im Bildarchiv Foto Marburg (23800 Negative), in den Beständen der Stiftung F. C. Gundlach sowie im Staatsarchiv Hamburg.

Quellen:

Konrad Helbig, Künstler-Datensatz 70055314, www.deutschefotothek.de mit umfangreicher Bibliografie

Raimund Wolfert, „Konrad Helbig", in: *Frankfurter Personenlexikon* (Onlineausgabe), https://frankfurter-personenlexikon.de/node/12345

Dank an Dr. Agnes Matthias von der Deutschen Fotothek für ihre Unterstützung bei dieser Einführung.

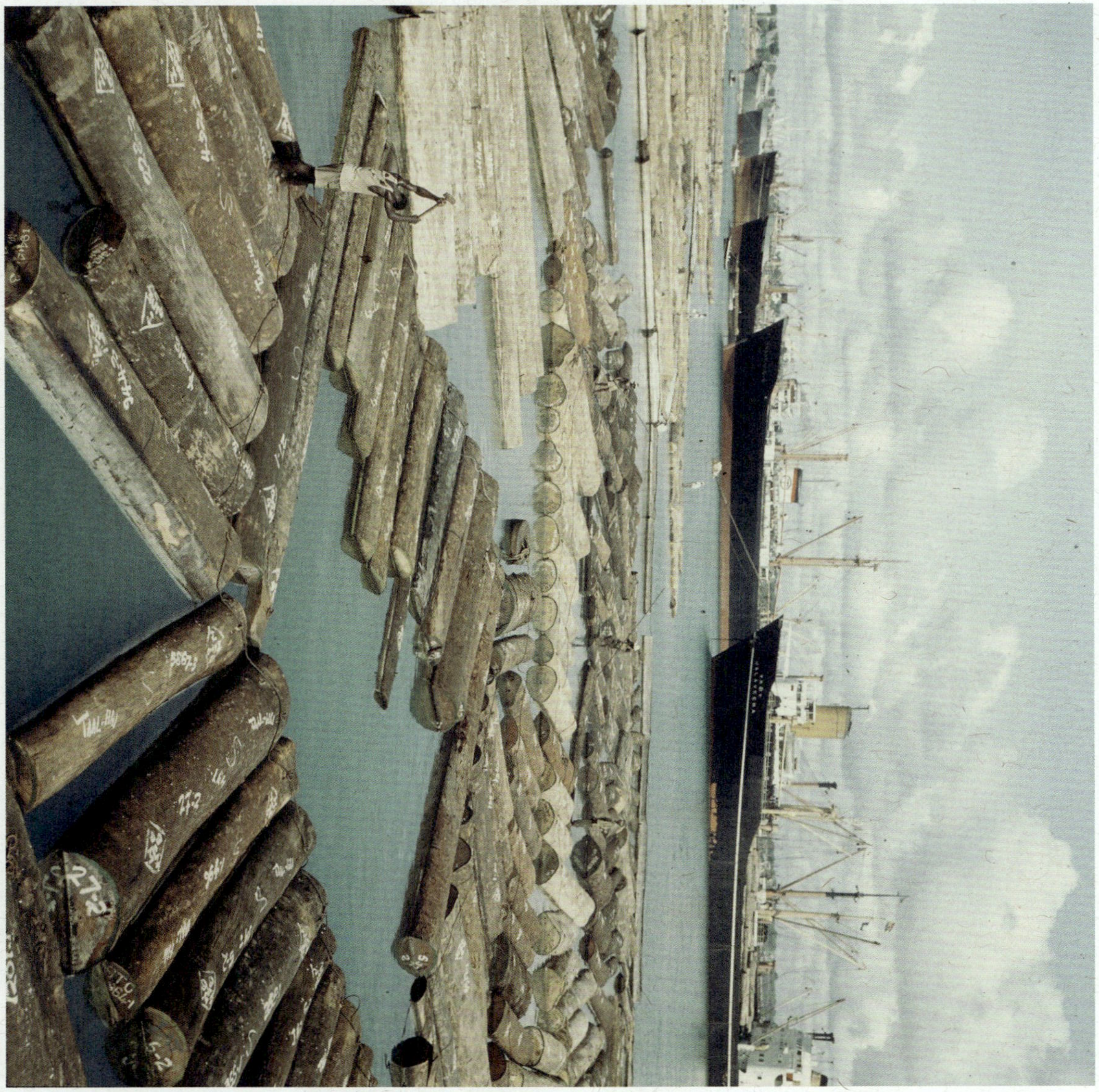

Konrad Helbig, Ghana-Reise, 07.04.1959, Takoradi

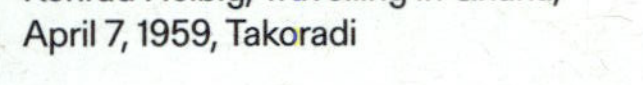

Konrad Helbig, Travelling in Ghana, April 7, 1959, Takoradi

KONRAD HELBIG, GHANA, 1959

KONRAD HELBIG, GHANA, 1959

Konrad Helbig, Traveling in Ghana, February 5, 1959, Tema, harbor

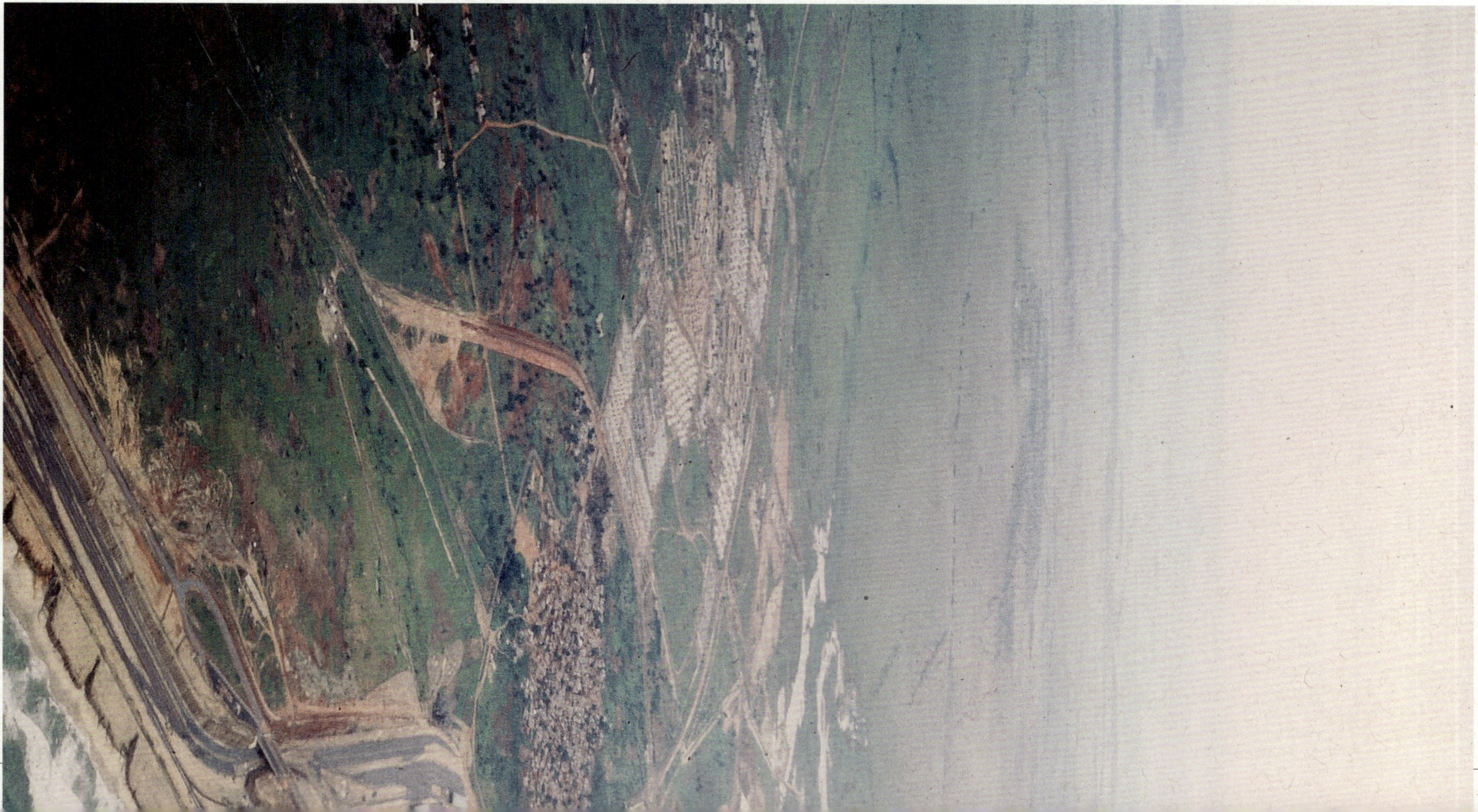

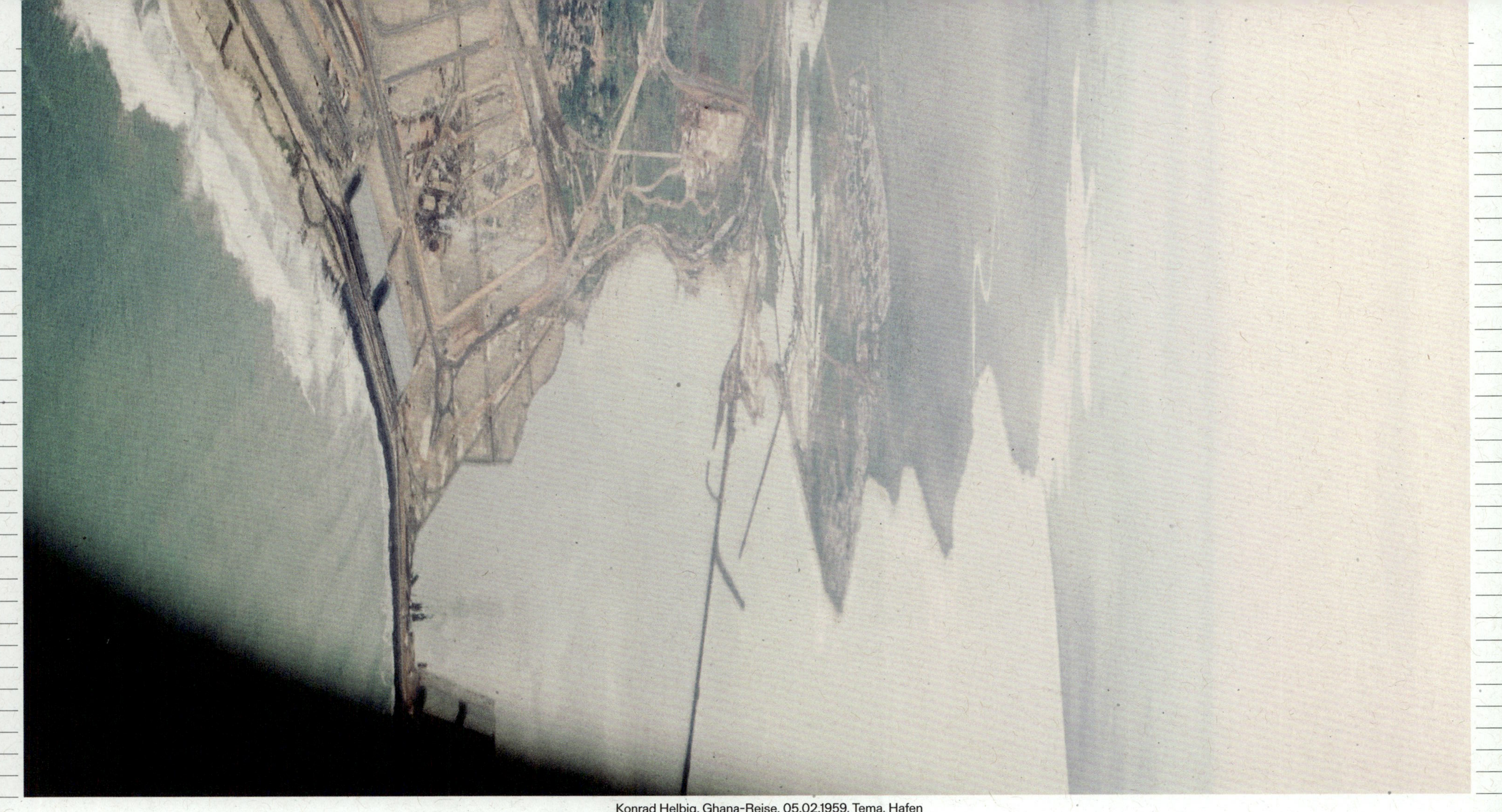

Konrad Helbig, Ghana-Reise, 05.02.1959, Tema, Hafen

Konrad Helbig, Traveling in Ghana, February 10, 1959, Tema

Konrad Helbig, Ghana-Reise, 10.02.1959, Tema

Konrad Helbig, Ghana-Reise, 10.02.1959, Tema

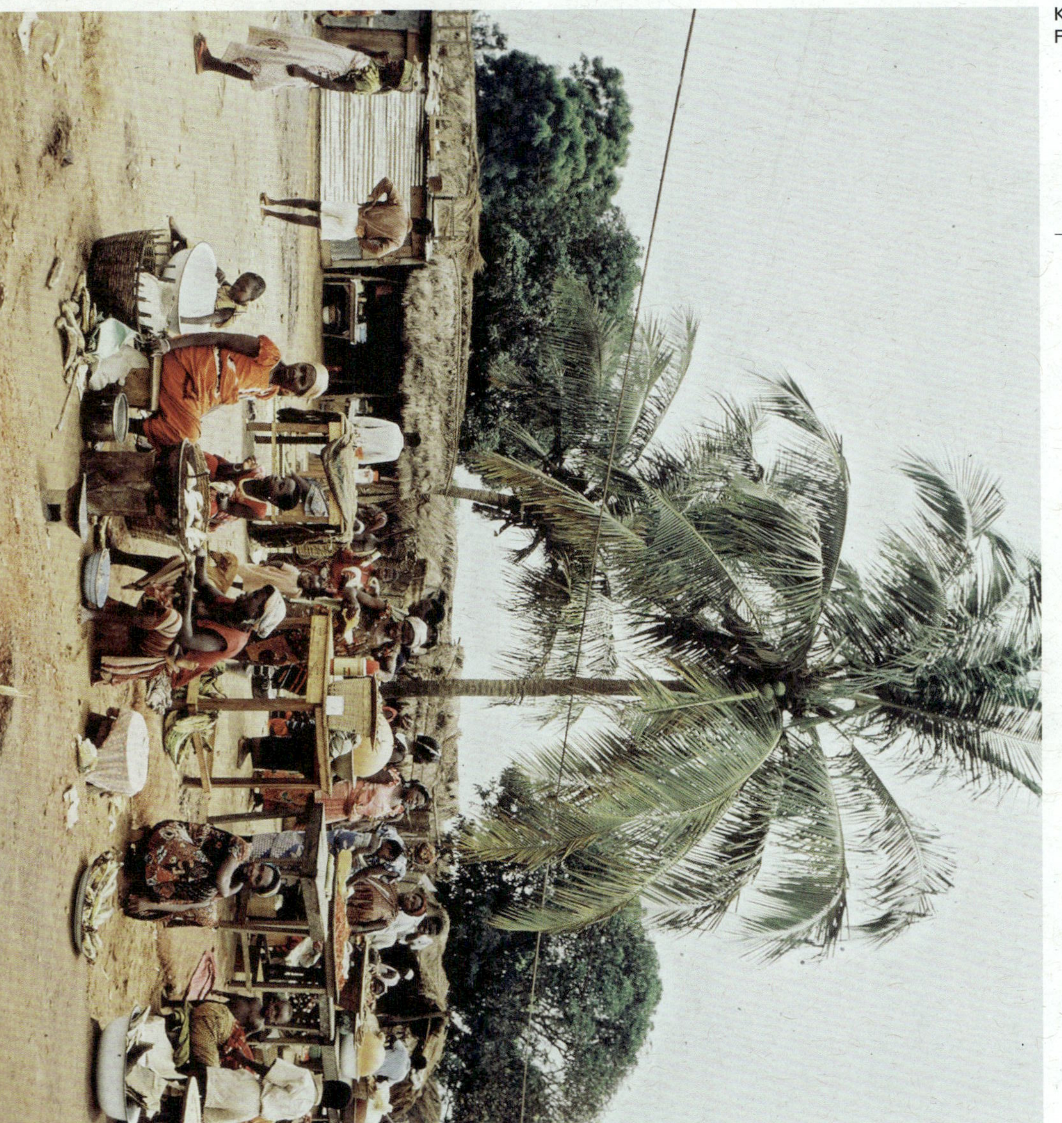

Konrad Helbig, Traveling in Ghana, February 10, 1959, Tema

KONRAD HELBIG, GHANA, 1959

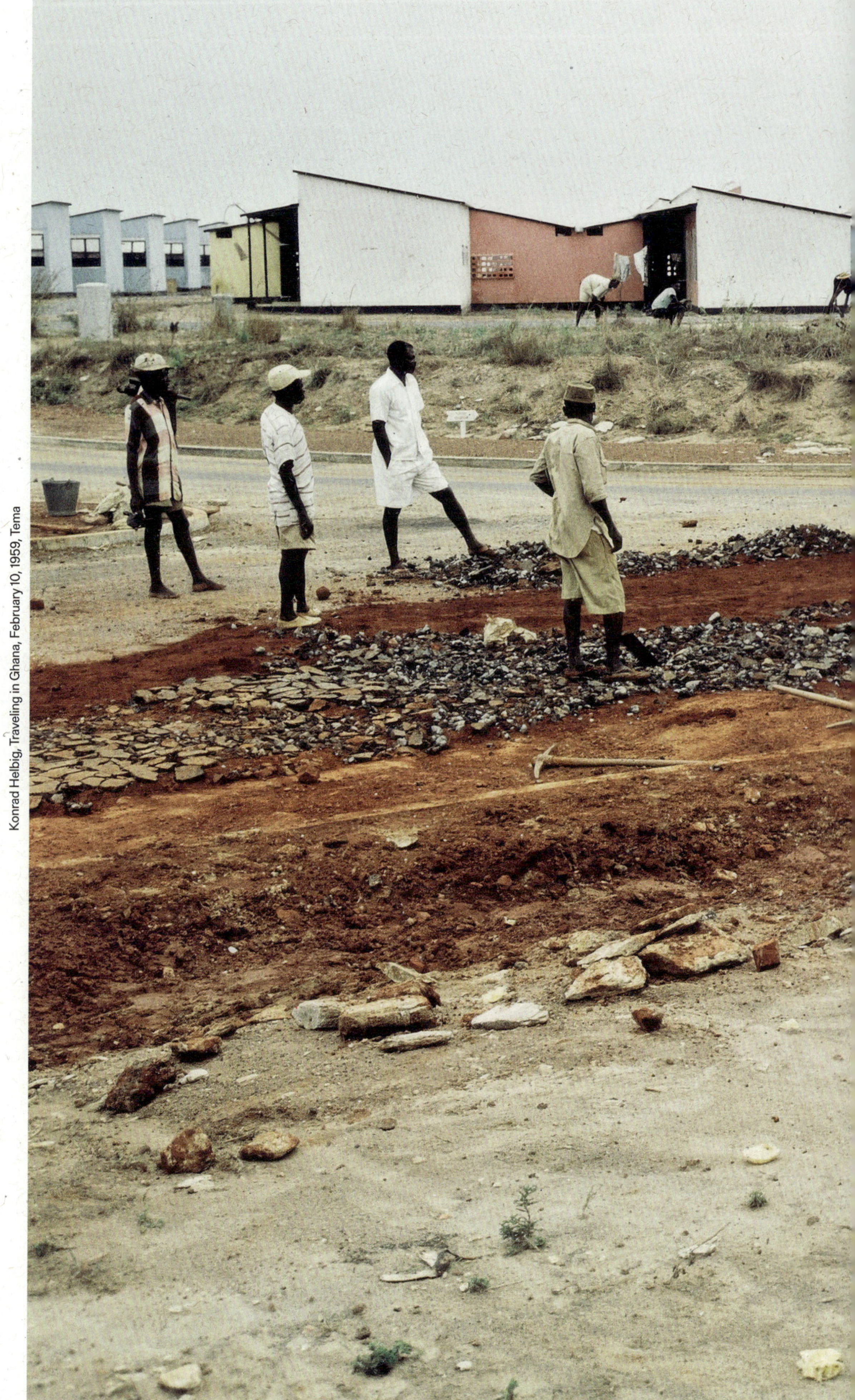

Konrad Helbig, Traveling in Ghana, February 10, 1959, Tema

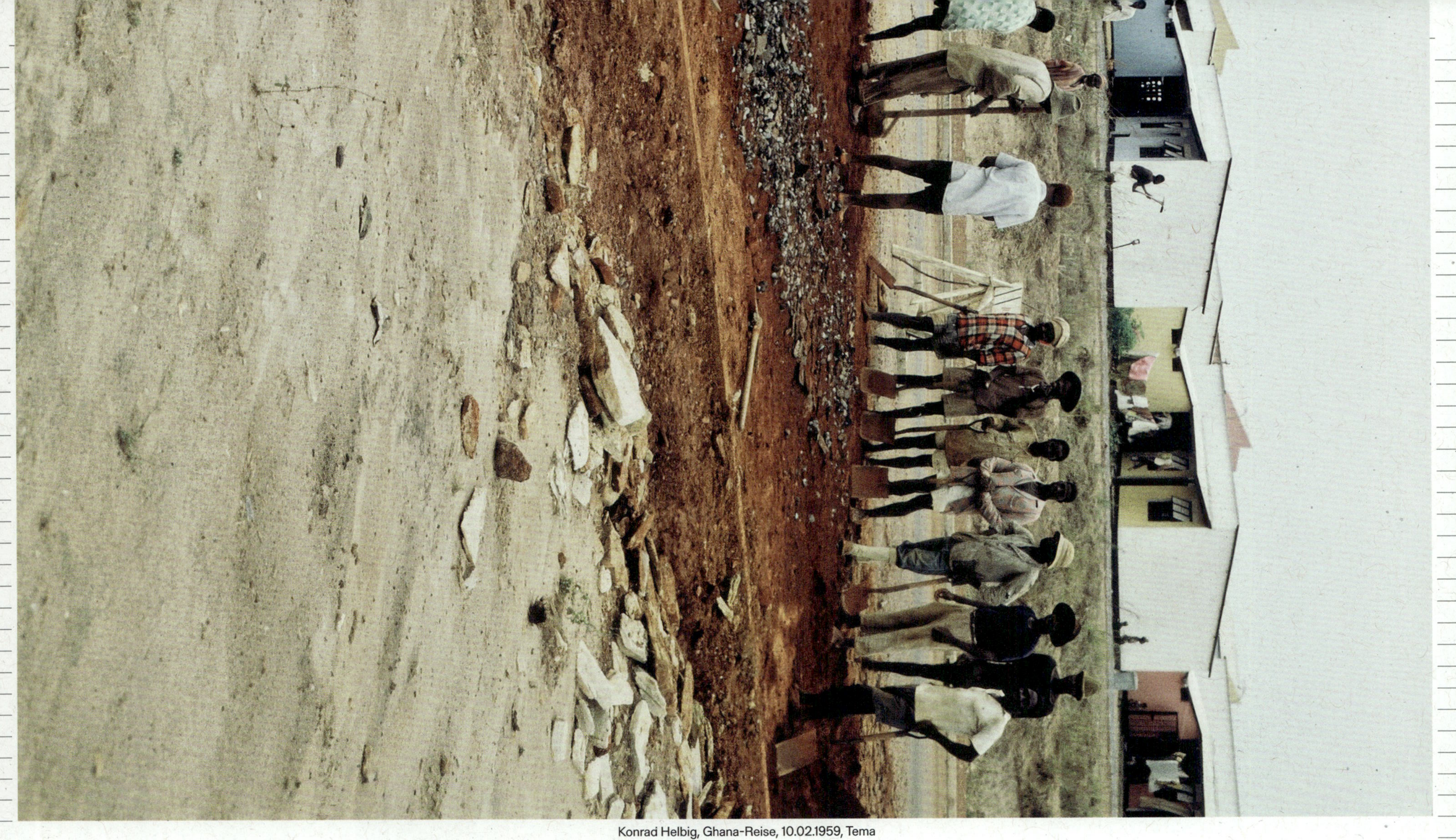

Konrad Helbig, Ghana-Reise, 10.02.1959, Tema

 KONRAD HELBIG, GHANA, 1959

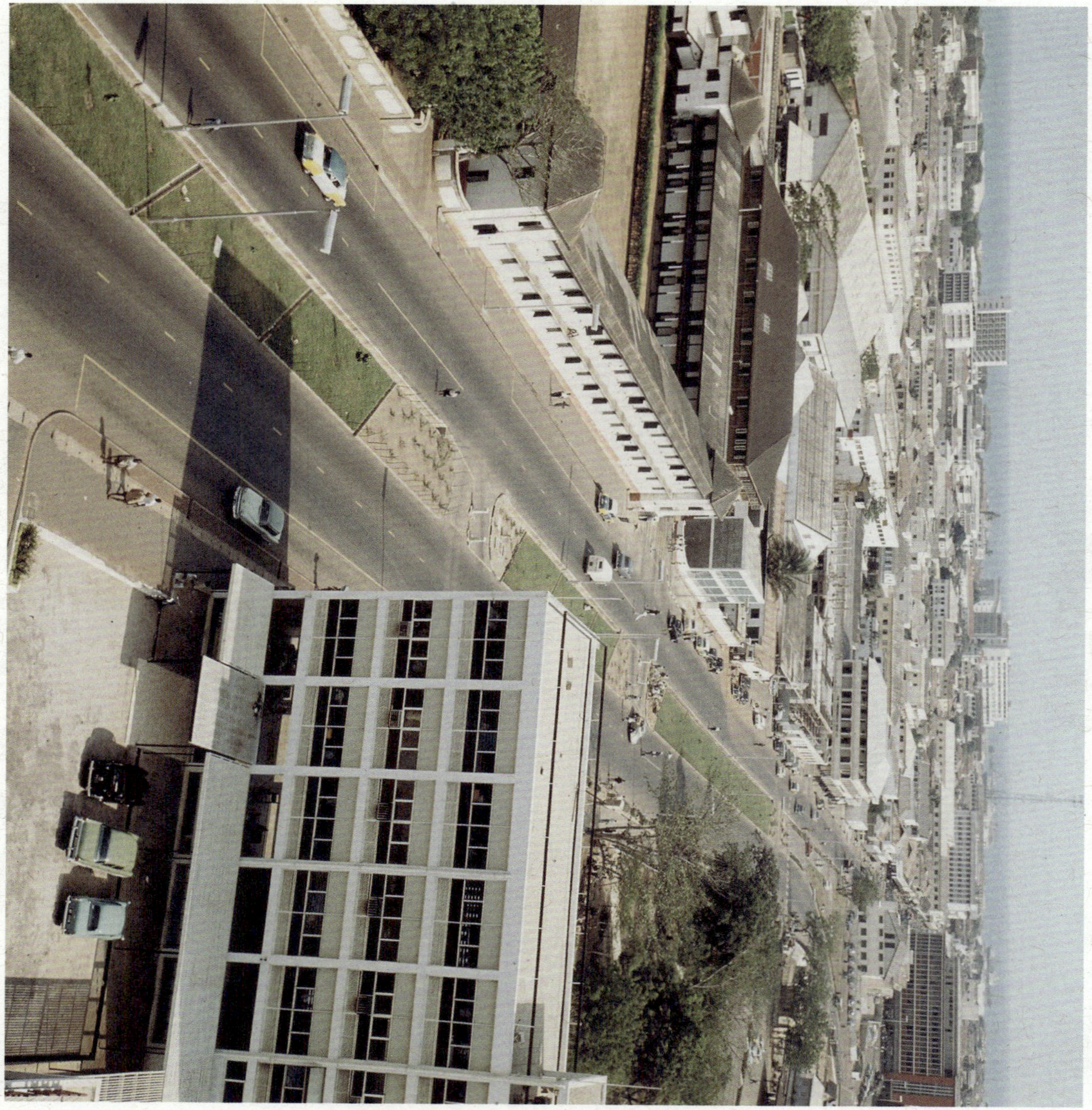

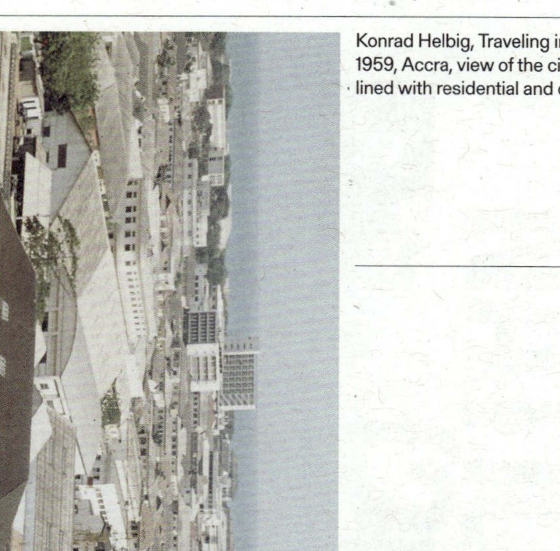

Konrad Helbig, Ghana-Reise, 23.02.1959, Accra, Blick auf die Stadt über eine von Wohn- und Geschäftshäusern gesäumte vierspurige Straße

Konrad Helbig, Traveling in Ghana, February 23, 1959, Accra, view of the city across a four-lane road lined with residential and commercial buildings

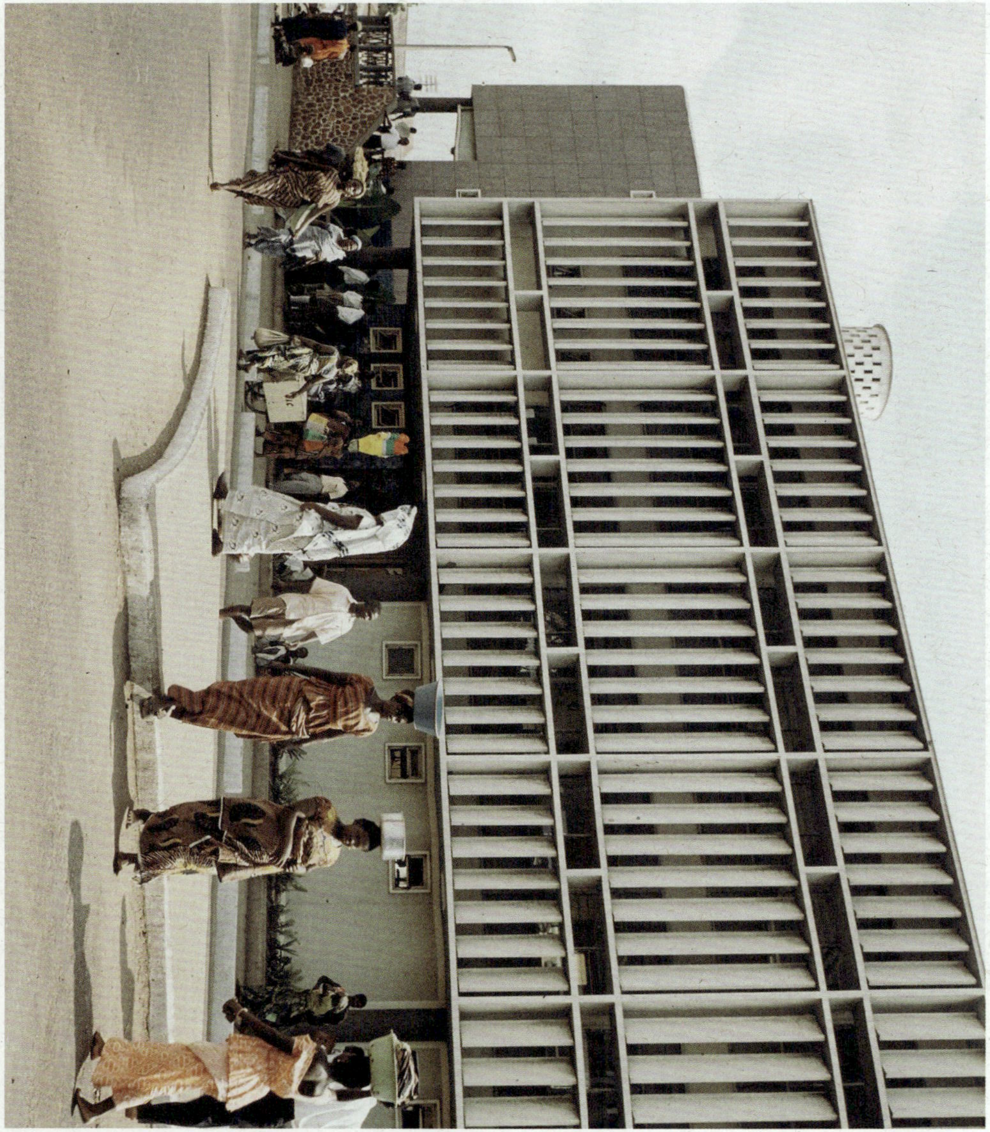

Konrad Helbig, Traveling in Ghana, February 1959, Accra; building: General Pcst Office

Konrad Helbig, Ghana-Reise, 02.1959, Accra, Bauwerk: General Post Office

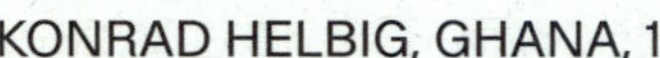

KONRAD HELBIG, GHANA, 1959

KONRAD HELBIG, GHANA, 1959

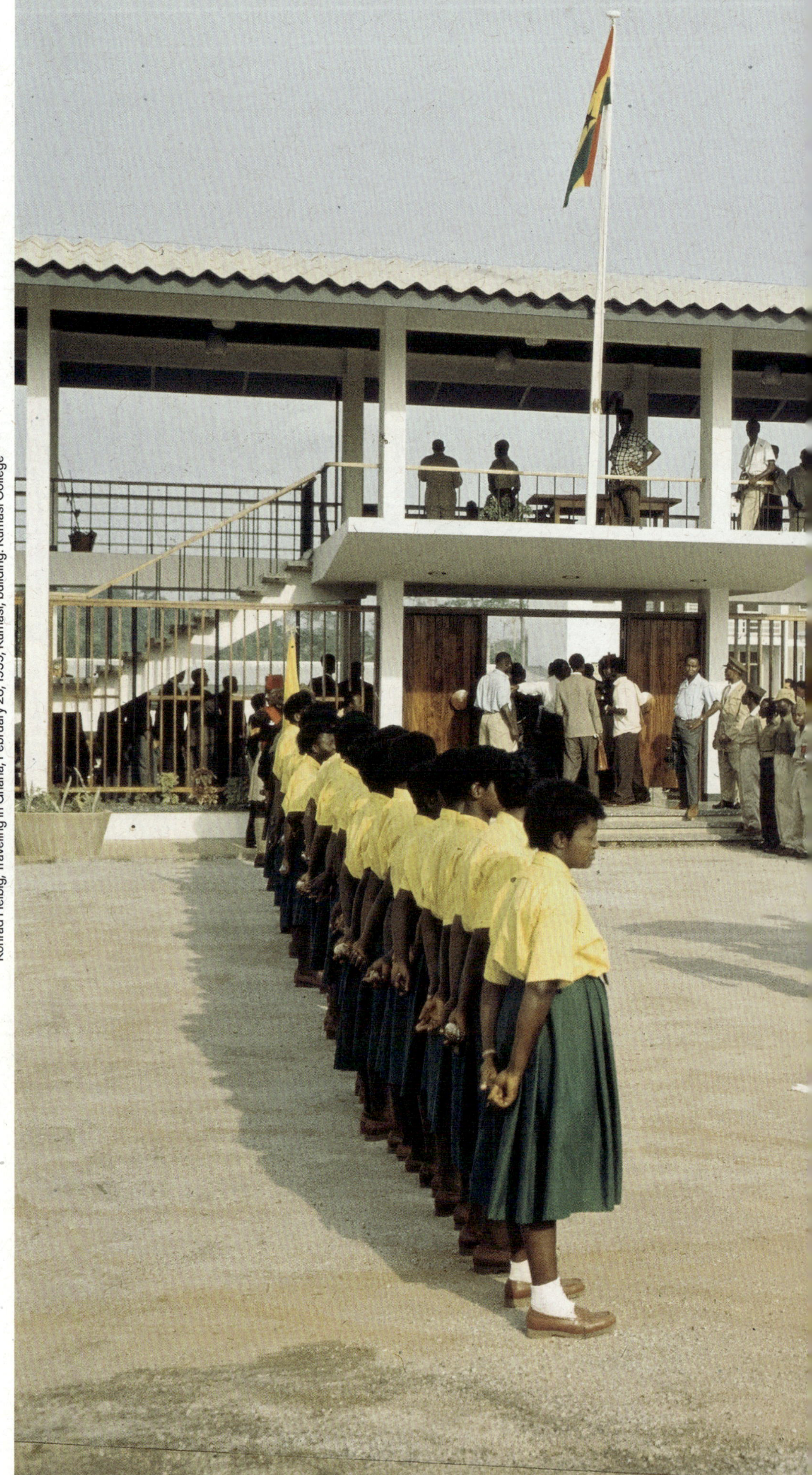

Konrad Helbig, Traveling in Ghana, February 28, 1959, Kumasi; building: Kumasi College

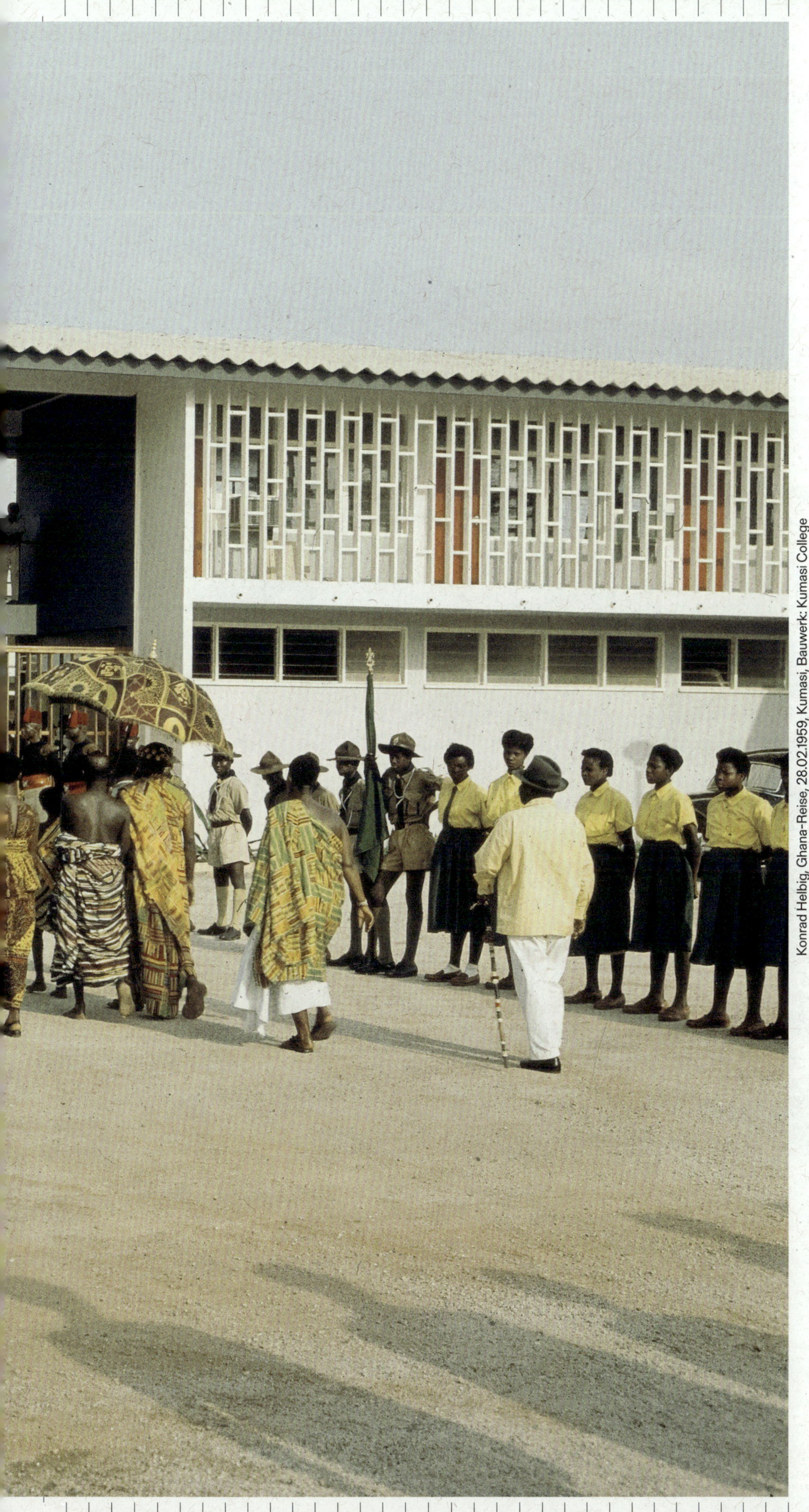

Konrad Helbig, Ghana-Reise, 28.02.1959, Kumasi, Bauwerk: Kumasi College

KONRAD HELBIG, GHANA, 1959

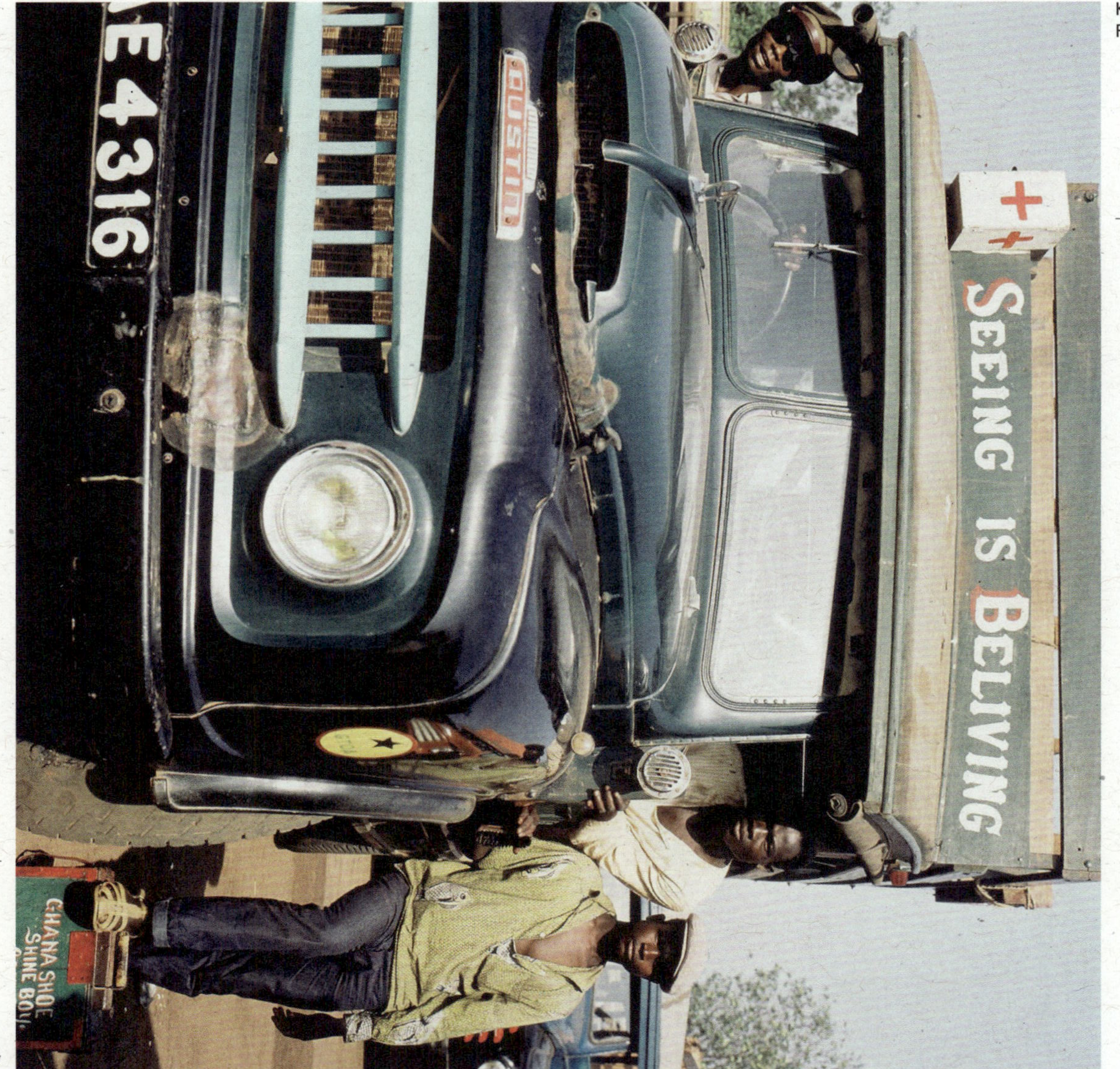

Konrad Helbig, Ghana-Reise, 02.1959, Accra, Lorry Station

Konrad Helbig, Traveling in Ghana, February 1959, Accra, Lorry Station

SECOND LOGIC

Doreen Mende

ZWEITE LOGIK

An archival logic can be of at least two kinds. Firstly, you can approach an archive with a precise enquiry based on dates, names, places, or contexts: for example, "GDR, Korea, internationalism, architecture, Bauhaus, Konrad Püschel." This data acts like a passport to an archive. Secondly, you may have this specific data, but you can't find what you're looking for. However, you find something else, near or in the vicinity of a document, that opens up a whole, previously unknown cosmos of friendships, manifestations, and images.

It was the second logic that brought this researcher to the governmental printing house in Tema, Ghana, which was built by the Leipzig collective led by civil engineer Kurt Fiedler and opened in September 1964 in honor of Ghana's President Kwame Nkrumah. The pan-African politician was the president of the first republic of an independent Ghana. She only came across this government printing press because she was looking for an architectural project by the Bauhaus-trained architect Konrad Püschel, who planned and realized the reconstruction of the city of Hamhung in North Korea in the early 1950s. She searched the archives in Geneva for that project because she had read that "during the 1954 Geneva conference on Korea and Indochina, East German minister president Otto Grotewohl told a North Korean delegate that his country would be willing to help rebuild one of the cities destroyed by the war."[1]

She was working in Geneva at the time and was in the United Nations Archives to research the 1954 Geneva conference, which had been held just around the corner from her workplace. The archives are located in the same building complex as the Palais des Nations. It is an extraterritorial site, where international, rather than Swiss law applies, as is the case with the free ports and the European Organization for Nuclear Research (CERN). It is beautifully situated on a hill on Geneva's Rive Droite (Right Bank) near Lac Leman. Entering the territory of the United Nations is like checking in at the airport with security and passport controls.

She had informed the archive's team of her research interest in advance. They provided her with a permit to enter the UN site. In the reading hall, the archivist in charge brought her a pile of documents on a mobile trolley. Archived

1. Young-Sun Hong, *Cold War Germany, the Third World, and the Global Humanitarian Regime* (Cambridge University Press, 2015), 60.

Es gibt mindestens zwei Arten der archivarischen Logik. Man kann, erstens, mit einer präzisen Anfrage in Form von Datumsangaben, Namen, Orten oder Kontexten an ein Archiv herantreten. Zum Beispiel: „DDR, Korea, Internationalismus, Architektur, Bauhaus, Konrad Püschel". Diese Daten sind dann gleichsam ein Reisepass für das Archiv. Oder, zweitens, man hat diese konkreten Daten, findet aber nicht, was man sucht. Allerdings findet man etwas anderes, in der Nähe oder in der Nachbarschaft eines Dokuments, das einen bisher unbekannten Kosmos von Freundschaften, Manifestationen und Bildern eröffnet.

Es war die zweite Logik, die die Forscherin zur Regierungsdruckerei in Tema (Ghana) führte, die von einem Leipziger Kollektiv um den Bauingenieur Kurt Fiedler gebaut und im September 1964 zu Ehren des ghanaischen Präsidenten Kwame Nkrumah eröffnet wurde. Der panafrikanische Politiker war der erste Präsident der ersten Republik des unabhängigen Ghana. Auf diese Staatsdruckerei war sie nur deshalb aufmerksam geworden, weil sie nach einem Bauprojekt des am Bauhaus ausgebildeten Architekten Konrad Püschel suchte, der in den frühen 1950er Jahren in Nordkorea den Wiederaufbau von Hamhung plante und realisierte. Sie suchte in Archiven in Genf nach diesem Projekt, weil sie bei Young-Sun Hong gelesen hatte: „Während der Genfer Indochinakonferenz von 1954 erklärte der DDR-Ministerpräsident Otto Grotewohl einem nordkoreanischen Delegierten, sein Land sei bereit, beim Wiederaufbau einer der durch den Krieg zerstörten Städte zu helfen."[1]

Sie arbeitete damals in Genf, so dass sie sich in den Archiven der Vereinten Nationen, ganz in der Nähe ihres Arbeitsplatzes, auf die Suche nach Informationen zur Genfer Konferenz von 1954 machen konnte. Die Archive befinden sich im selben Gebäudekomplex wie der Palais des Nations. Es handelt sich dabei um ein extraterritoriales Gelände, auf dem nicht Schweizer Recht gilt, sondern internationales Recht wie in den Freihäfen und der Europäischen Organisation für Kernforschung (CERN). Es ist wunderschön gelegen, ein wenig auf einem Hügel, an der *rive droite de Genève* in der Nähe des Lac Leman. Wer das Territorium der Vereinten Nationen betritt, durchläuft eine Art Check-in mit Sicherheits- und Passkontrollen wie am Flughafen.

Sie hatte das Archivteam im Voraus über ihr Forschungsinteresse informiert. Daraufhin erhielt sie eine Genehmigung für den Zugang zum

1. Young-Sun Hong, *Cold War Germany, the Third World, and the Global Humanitarian Regime*, New York u. a.: Cambridge University Press 2015, S. 60.

2. The author would like to thank Thomas Flierl for sharing information about the magazine and Bruno Flierl, who was its editor-in-chief between 1962 and 1964.

newspapers and magazines, correspondence, communiqués, minutes, etc. The pile of material also contained the magazine *Deutsche Architektur*, published by the Bauakademie der Deutschen Demokratischen Republik, which was founded in 1951 by Kurt Liebknecht (Karl Liebknecht's nephew) on behalf of the East German government. She was previously unaware of this magazine, which has had various names over the years. From 1952 to 1974, it was called *Deutsche Architektur*, then *Architektur der DDR*, and between 1990 and 1991, *Architektur*.[2]

The researcher found nothing about the cooperation of architects between North Korea and the GDR in the early 1950s. Not even a note or a minute documenting the presence of Grotewohl in Geneva. But following the second archive logic, she looked through the pile of issues covering a decade of construction projects in the Czechoslovak Socialist Republic, Poland, Vietnam, Zanzibar . . . and by sheer coincidence, she came across a four-page report in *Deutsche Architektur* 9 (1964), pages 540–43, on the government printing house in Ghana. It documents its construction in Tema, a city on the Bight of Benin and the Atlantic coast of Ghana, by a collective from VEB Zentrales Projektierungsbüro [Publicly Owned Enterprise Central Design Bureau] "Polygraph" in Leipzig since 1961. On the occasion of Nkrumah's birthday on September 21, 1964, the representatives of the GDR handed the building over to the Ghanaian government. Once again, she learned something about the GDR (a country she happened to have been born into), not only outside Germany but also quite by chance. As had often happened before.

At the time, in 1964, when the report on the government printing house in Tema was published, the editor-in-chief of the magazine was the architect and critic Bruno Flierl. She had tried to organize an interview with him in Berlin, but the Covid global pandemic didn't allow the meeting to take place. There was hardly anything to be found on the Tema printing house except in *Architekturprojekte der DDR im Ausland: Bauten, Akteure und kulturelle Transferprozesse* (2016–18) at the Historische Forschungsstelle des Leibniz-Instituts für Raumbezogene Sozialforschung (IRS) in Erkner near Berlin. Moreover, the excellent compendium *Architecture in Global Socialism: Eastern Europe, West Africa, and*

UN-Gelände. Die verantwortliche Archivarin brachte ihr einen Stapel von Dokumenten auf einem mobilen Wagen in den Lesesaal. Archivierte Zeitungen und Zeitschriften, Korrespondenzen, Communiqués, Protokolle und so weiter. Im Materialstapel befand sich auch die Zeitschrift *Deutsche Architektur*, herausgegeben von der Bauakademie der Deutschen Demokratischen Republik, welche im Auftrag der Regierung 1951 von Kurt Liebknecht (einem Neffen von Karl Liebknecht) gegründet wurde. Sie wusste bisher nichts von dieser Zeitschrift, die im Lauf der Zeit unter verschiedenen Titeln erschien. Von 1952 bis 1974 hieß sie *Deutsche Architektur*, dann *Architektur der DDR* und zwischen 1990 und 1991 nur noch *Architektur*.[2]

Über die Zusammenarbeit von Architekten in Nordkorea und der DDR in den frühen 1950er Jahren fand die Forscherin nichts im Archiv. Nicht einmal eine Notiz oder ein Protokoll, das die Anwesenheit von Grotewohl in Genf dokumentiert hätte. Aber gemäß der zweiten Archivlogik durchsuchte sie den Stapel von Ausgaben, die ein Jahrzehnt von Bauprojekten in der Tschechoslowakischen Sozialistischen Republik, in Polen, Vietnam, Sansibar zeigten ... In der *Deutschen Architektur* 9/1964 stieß sie dann zufällig auf einen vierseitigen Bericht. Er dokumentiert den Bau der Regierungsdruckerei in Tema, einer Stadt am Golf von Benin und der Atlantikküste Ghanas, welcher seit 1961 von einem Kollektiv des VEB Zentrales Projektierungsbüro "Polygraph" aus Leipzig realisiert wurde. Anlässlich Nkrumahs Geburtstag am 21. September 1964 übergaben die Vertreter der DDR das Gebäude an die ghanaische Regierung (S. 540–543). Wieder einmal erfuhr sie etwas über die DDR (das Land, in dem sie geboren worden war), und das nicht nur außerhalb von Deutschland, sondern ohne eigentlich danach gesucht zu haben. So war es ihr schon oft ergangen.

Als 1964 der Bericht über die staatliche Druckerei in Tema veröffentlicht wurde, war der Chefredakteur der Zeitschrift der Architekt und Kritiker Bruno Flierl. Sie hatte versucht, ein Interview mit ihm in Berlin zu organisieren, doch die weltweite Covid-Pandemie machte ein Treffen unmöglich. Über die Druckerei in Tema war sonst kaum etwas zu finden, außer dem Forschungsprojekt „Architekturprojekte der DDR im Ausland. Bauten, Akteure und kulturelle Transferprozesse“ (2016–2018) an der Historischen Forschungsstelle des Leibniz-Instituts für Raumbezogene Sozialforschung (IRS) in Erkner bei Berlin. Das

2. Vielen Dank an Thomas Flierl für die aufschlussreichen Gespräche über die Zeitschrift und über Bruno Flierl, der von 1962 bis 1964 deren Chefredakteur war.

the Middle East in the Cold War (2020) by Łukasz Stanek missed the Tema printing house, most likely because the building did not exist anymore. How to engage with absent material, whose traces nonetheless constitute forms of immaterial knowledge with relevance for the present?

The Benjaminian encounter with the neighbor of what was sought but not found prepared the ground for a new research case. The coming together of neighborhoods in the archive led the researcher to the Government Printing Press, in Tema, Ghana. It was then an obvious step to invite Kwasi Ohene-Ayeh and his friends to explore the remnants, memories, and printed matter of the place since 2020. The research continues.

herausragende Kompendium *Architecture in Global Socialism: Eastern Europe, West Africa, and the Middle East in the Cold War* (2020) von Łukasz Stanek dokumentiert die Druckerei Tema nicht, wahrscheinlich weil das Gebäude nicht mehr existiert. Wie geht man vor, wenn das Material fehlt, aber Spuren zu einem immateriellen Wissen führen, welches für die Gegenwart bedeutsam ist?

Die Benjamin'sche Begegnung mit dem Nachbarn dessen, was gesucht, aber nicht gefunden wurde, legte den Grundstein für eine neue Forschungsfallstudie. Die Nachbarschaften im Archiv führten die Forscherin zur ghanaischen Regierungsdruckerei in Tema, und so lag es nahe, Kwasi Ohene-Ayeh und seine Freunde einzuladen, die Bruchstücke, Erinnerungen und Drucksachen des Ortes seit 2020 zu erforschen. Die Forschung geht weiter.

GHANA: TEMA GOVERNMENT PRINTING PRESS

Reprint from *Deutsche Architektur* 9 (1964)

GHANA: REGIERUNGS-DRUCKEREI IN TEMA

Nachdruck aus *Deutsche Architektur*, Heft 9 (1964)

Civil engineer Kurt Fiedler, BDA (Association of German Architects)

VEB Industrieprojektierung Leipzig
Structural engineering concern specializing in the printing industry

Overall construction management:
Kurt Fiedler, BDA, civil engineer

Head of functionality and design:
Hermann Pape, BDA, architect
Wolfgang Stagun, BDA, qualified engineer

Design team:
Ronald Brandt, BDA, civil engineer
Erich Hoffmann, BDA, qualified engineer
Walter Süßkind, BDA, architect

Statics and construction team:
Dieter Bartsch, qualified engineer
Heinz Kober, KdT (Chamber of Engineers), civil engineer
Peter Kossiel, civil engineer
Willy Szyszka, civil engineer

1. Model of the entire system

2. Site plan, 1:2000
1 Production building (aisles I–IV)
2 Transformer station
3 Editorial and administration building
4 Dining room
5 Kitchen
6 WC, washroom, and changing rooms
7 Garages
8 Covered parking, gatehouse

3. Construction work on the editorial and administrative building

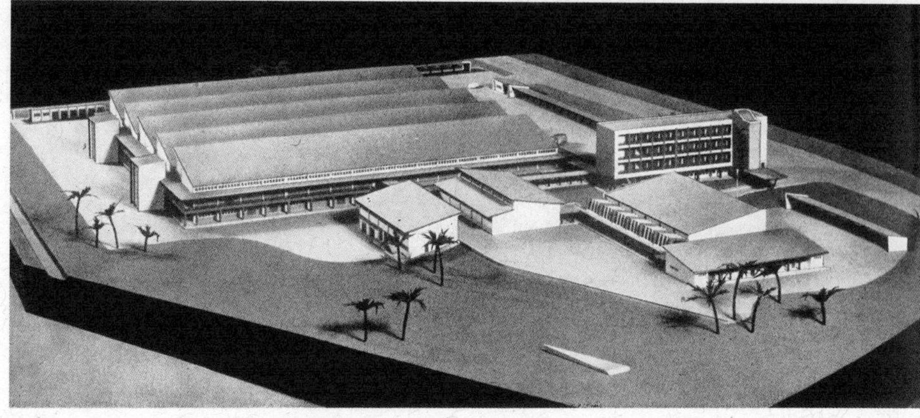
1

Ghana ■

Regierungsdruckerei in Tema

Bauingenieur Kurt Fiedler, BDA

VEB Industrieprojektierung Leipzig
Bautechnischer Spezialprojektant für die grafische Industrie

Bautechnische Gesamtplanung:
Bauingenieur Kurt Fiedler, BDA

Verantwortlich für Funktion und Gestaltung:
Baumeister Hermann Pape, BDA
Dipl.-Ing. Wolfgang Stagun, BDA

Mitarbeiter Entwurf:
Bauingenieur Ronald Brandt, BDA
Dipl.-Ing. Erich Hoffmann, BDA
Baumeister Walter Süßkind, BDA

Mitarbeiter Statik und Konstruktion:
Dipl.-Ing. Djeter Bartsch
Bauingenieur Heinz Kober, KDT
Bauingenieur Peter Kossiel
Bauingenieur Willy Szyszka

1
Modellaufnahme der Gesamtanlage

2
Lageplan 1 : 2000
1 Produktionsgebäude (Schiffe I–V)
2 Trafostation
3 Redaktions- und Verwaltungsgebäude
4 Speisesaal
5 Küche
6 WC-, Wasch- und Umkleideräume
7 Werkgaragen
8 Kraftwagenunterstellräume, Pförtnergebäude

3
Bauarbeiten am Redaktions- und Verwaltungsgebäude

540

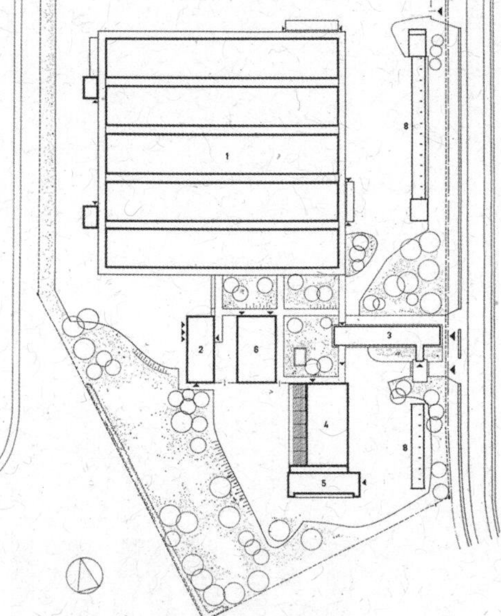

Bauingenieur Kurt Fiedler, BDA

VEB Industrieprojektierung Leipzig
Bautechnischer Spezialprojektant für die grafische Industrie

Bautechnische Gesamtplanung:
Bauingenieur Kurt Fiedler, BDA

Verantwortlich für Funktion und Gestaltung:
Baumeister Hermann Pape, BDA
Dipl.-Ing. Wolfgang Stagun, BDA

Mitarbeiter Entwurf:
Bauingenieur Ronald Brandt, BDA
Dipl.-Ing. Erich Hoffmann, BDA
Baumeister Walter Süßkind, BDA

Mitarbeiter Statik und Konstruktion:
Dipl.-Ing. Dieter Bartsch
Bauingenieur Heinz Kober, KDT
Bauingenieur Peter Kossiel
Bauingenieur Willy Szyszka

1. Modellaufnahme der Gesamtanlage

2. Lageplan 1 : 2000
1 Produktionsgebäude (Schiffe I–V)
2 Trafostation
3 Redaktions- und Verwaltungsgebäude
4 Speisesaal
5 Küche
6 WC-, Wasch- und Umkleideräume
7 Werkgaragen
8 Kraftwagenunterstellräume, Pförtnergebäude

3. Bauarbeiten am Redaktions- und Verwaltungsgebäude

On September 21, 1964, in honor of the birthday of the president of the Republic of Ghana, Kwame Nkrumah, a large-scale printing facility in Tema, the new and upwardly striving port city on the Atlantic coast, was handed over to the Ghanaian government—the Ministry of Information and Broadcasting—and put into operation. This large printing works was planned and delivered as a complete facility by the chief design engineer of the East German state-owned company VEB Zentrales Projektierungsbüro "Polygraph" Leipzig. The construction project was developed by VEB Industrieprojektierung Leipzig, the structural engineering concern specializing in polygraph printing.

The technological and architectural design of the sub-elements was carried out in line with a planning and construction schedule coordinated with the contracting partner and the Ghana National Construction Company (GNCC) in the period from March 1961 to the beginning of December 1962. Building work began in June 1962.

The structural planning was complicated by the fact that the availability of materials in the country needed to be clarified within a relatively short space of time. A painstaking study of the local climatic conditions was also required to come up with the perfect structural designs and functions. Sun, wind, rain, temperature, and humidity were all key considerations in the design process. A further issue was compliance with the building laws applicable to Tema. The British reinforced concrete regulations and weights and measures system were used as a basis for the static and design work. The civil engineer was familiar, from other printing works he had already designed, with certain key problems associated with the design of large printing plants in tropical areas with warm and humid climates (see issue no. 10, 1962).

SITE CONDITION

The building plot is located at the southern tip of the industrial area earmarked for the port city of Tema at an important point of convergence for residential and industrial developments, the port area, and the main road to Accra (the country's capital). This location was chosen by Tema's city planning department because

Am 21. September 1964 wurde anläßlich des Geburtstages des Präsidenten der Republik Ghana, Nkrumah, in Tema, der neuen, aufwärtsstrebenden Hafenstadt an der Atlantikküste, ein polygrafischer Großbetrieb an die ghanesische Regierung – Ministerium für Information und Rundfunk – übergeben und in Betrieb genommen. Diese Großdruckerei wurde als komplette Anlage von dem Generalprojektanten VEB Zentrales Projektierungsbüro „Polygraph" Leipzig projektiert und ausgeliefert. Die Ausarbeitung des bautechnischen Projektes lag in den Händen des bautechnischen Spezialprojektanten für den Industriezweig Polygraphie VEB Industrieprojektierung Leipzig.

Die technologischen und bautechnischen Projektierungen der Teilobjekte erfolgten nach einem mit dem Auftraggeber und dem staatlichen Baubetrieb G. N. C. C. abgestimmten Projektierungs- und Bauablaufplan in dem Zeitraum März 1961 bis Anfang Dezember 1962. Mit dem Bau wurde im Juni 1962 begonnen.

Die Problematik für die bautechnische Projektierung bestand darin, daß eine umfassende Klärung der Materialsituation des Landes in relativ kurzer Zeit herbeigeführt werden mußte. Im weiteren mußten die örtlichen klimatischen Verhältnisse genauestens studiert werden, um einwandfreie bautechnische Konstruktionen und Funktionen finden zu können. Sonne, Wind, Regen, Temperatur und Luftfeuchte waren für die Entwurfsbearbeitungen stark zu beachtende Faktoren. Weiterhin mußten die für Tema zutreffenden Baugesetze beachtet werden. Für die statischen und konstruktiven Bearbeitungen waren die englischen Stahlbetonbestimmungen als auch das englische Maß- und Gewichtssystem Grundlage. Mit gewissen Hauptproblemen, die für eine Projektierung von grafischen Großbetrieben in tropischen Gebieten mit feuchtwarmem Klima stehen, war der bautechnische Projektant durch andere, bereits von ihm projektierte grafische Betriebe vertraut (s. auch Heft 10/1962).

LAGEPLANSITUATION

Das Baugrundstück liegt im Südzipfel des für die Hafenstadt Tema ausgewiesenen Industriegeländes an einem wichtigen Berührungspunkt zwischen Wohnbebauung, Industriebebauung, Hafengelände und der Hauptstraße nach Accra (Hauptstadt des Landes). Dieser Standort war deswegen von der Stadtplanung Temas gewählt worden, weil die zu bauende Regierungsdruckerei den

Construction work

The construction project "Tema Government Printing Press in Ghana" comprised the sub-elements:

Site planning
Utility lines
Irrigation and drainage, road construction
Production building (aisles I–V)
Transformer station
Editorial and administration building
Dining room (multipurpose room) and kitchen
Toilet, washing and changing rooms
Factory garages
Vehicle shelters and porter's building
Fencing, terrace and parapet walls, covered walkways

3

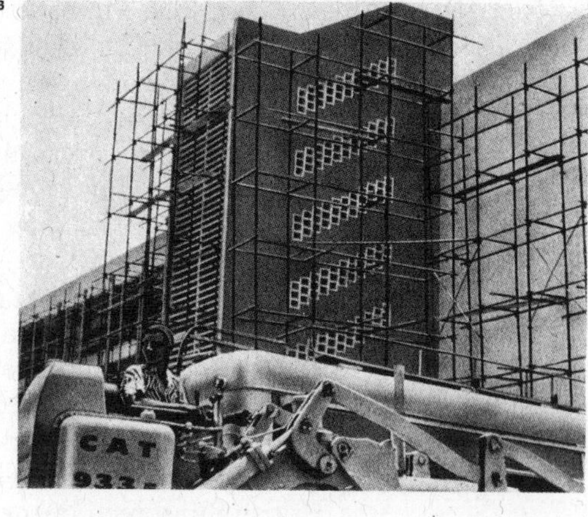

Am 21. September 1964 wurde anläßlich des Geburtstages des Präsidenten der Republik Ghana, Nkrumah, in Tema, der neuen, aufwärtsstrebenden Hafenstadt an der Atlantikküste, ein polygrafischer Großbetrieb an die ghanesische Regierung – Ministerium für Information und Rundfunk – übergeben und in Betrieb genommen. Diese Großdruckerei wurde als komplette Anlage von dem Generalprojektanten VEB Zentrales Projektierungsbüro „Polygraph" Leipzig projektiert und ausgeliefert. Die Ausarbeitung des bautechnischen Projektes lag in Händen des bautechnischen Spezialprojektanten für den Industriezweig Polygraphie VEB Industrieprojektierung Leipzig.

Die technologischen und bautechnischen Projektierungen der Teilobjekte erfolgten nach einem mit dem Auftraggeber und dem staatlichen Baubetrieb G. N. C. C. abgestimmten Projektierungs- und Bauablaufplan in dem Zeitraum März 1961 bis Anfang Dezember 1962. Mit dem Bau wurde im Juni 1962 begonnen.

Die Problematik für die bautechnische Projektierung bestand darin, daß eine umfassende Klärung der Materialsituation des Landes in relativ kurzer Zeit herbeigeführt werden mußte. Im weiteren mußten die örtlichen klimatischen Verhältnisse genauestens studiert werden, um einwandfreie bautechnische Konstruktionen und Funktionen finden zu können. Sonne, Wind, Regen, Temperatur und Luftfeuchte waren für die Entwurfsbearbeitungen stark zu beachtende Faktoren. Weiterhin mußten die für Tema zutreffenden Baugesetze beachtet werden. Für die statischen und konstruktiven Bearbeitungen waren die englischen Stahlbetonbestimmungen als auch das englische Maß- und Gewichtssystem Grundlage. Mit gewissen Hauptproblemen, die für eine Projektierung von grafischen Großbetrieben in tropischen Gebieten mit feuchtwarmem Klima stehen, war der bautechnische Projektant durch andere, bereits von ihm projektierte grafische Betriebe vertraut (s. auch Heft 10/1962).

Lageplansituation

Das Baugrundstück liegt im Südzipfel des für die Hafenstadt Tema ausgewiesenen Industriegeländes an einem wichtigen Berührungspunkt zwischen Wohnbebauung, Industriebebauung, Hafengelände und der Hauptstraße nach Accra (Hauptstadt des Landes). Dieser Standort war deswegen von der Stadtplanung Temas gewählt worden, weil die zu bauende Regierungsdruckerei den städtebaulichen und architektonischen Akzent für dieses Gebiet darstellen sollte. Außerdem war die Standortwahl auch von versorgungs- und verkehrstechnischen Überlegungen abhängig gemacht worden.

Das Baugelände liegt westlich der Straße Nr. 36 und soll westlich von der in der Planung befindlichen Auto-Ringstraße begrenzt werden. Es fällt sehr stark von Südost nach Nordwest ab. Die Zufahrten waren an der Straße Nr. 36 anzuordnen.

Entwurf und Gestaltung

Seit langem schon ist für die grafische Industrie der Kompaktbau die bauliche Anlage, die für die Gesamtfunktion der Technologie ausgezeichnete ökonomische Ergebnisse bringt. Auch in den Tropen ist der Kompaktbau unter besonderen Bedingungen realisierbar. Die klimatischen Verhältnisse der Tropen verlangen eine sehr gute natürliche Querlüftung aller Räume des Kompaktbaus, da es unökonomisch wäre, für die Produktionshallen zentrale Lüftungs- oder gar Klimaanlagen vorzusehen. Lediglich in verschiedenen Abteilungen der Produktion sind örtliche Klimageräte (Airconditions) oder örtliche Be- und Entlüftungsanlagen in der fünfschiffigen Produktionshalle angeordnet worden. Um eine „Aufheizung" im Innern des Produktionsgebäudes durch direkte Sonneneinstrahlung zu vermeiden, mußte das Gebäude in der Längsachse Ost–West orientiert werden, da die stärkste Sonneneinstrahlung von Osten und Westen erfolgt. Der südliche Sonnenstand ist unproblematisch, da dieser senkrecht ist. Für die natürliche Durchlüftung der Gebäude ist die Hauptwindrichtung maßgebend, das heißt, die Fensteranordnung mußte sich danach richten.

Die in der Regenzeit einsetzenden sehr starken Regengüsse verlangten wohlüberlegte Dachkonstruktionen mit großen Dachüberständen. Die Windrichtung und die Hauptregenrichtung waren dabei mitbestimmende Faktoren. Dadurch entstanden die eigenwillig anmutenden Dachformen bei verschiedenen Gebäuden.

Für die Hallenschiffe des Produktionsgebäudes sollten nach der Aufgabenstellung des Generalprojektanten sehr gute natürliche Lichtverhältnisse geschaffen werden. Die Orientierung der großen Louvres-Fenster mußte nach Nord-Nordost erfolgen, um ein den ganzen Tag über kontinuierliches Tageslicht zu garantieren.

Die Dächer des Produktionsgebäudes sind mit schallschluckenden, abgehängten Zwischendecken versehen und entsprechend durchlüftet. Ein Wärmedämmstoff, der unter der oberen Dachhaut (Wellaluminium) angeordnet ist, hat außerdem die Funktion, die Trommelwirkung bei Regen zu mindern. Im Gebäudeinnern sind im Mittel 5 bis 6 °C niedrigere Temperaturen gemessen worden als außerhalb der Hallen. Dies ist durch die vorgesehene Dachkonstruktion im Zusammenspiel mit der Gebäudequerlüftung erreicht worden.

Konstruktion

Der monolithische Stahlbetonskelettbau wird in Ghana bevorzugt. Er muß den Forderungen, die in den „Westafrikanischen Baubestimmungen" festgelegt sind, entsprechen. Die Wandausfachungen werden mit Betonblöcken oder Betonhohlsteinen ausgeführt. Die Fundamentierung erfolgte auf verwittertem Gneis und richtete sich nach den für Erdbebengebiete festgelegten Bestimmungen, die in der obenangeführten Bauordnung enthalten sind. Es ist landesüblich, daß die dachhauttragenden Konstruktionselemente aus Mahagoniholz vorgesehen werden. Das im Bauwerk verwendete Holz, das tragende Funktionen übernehmen muß, wird gegen Termiten, Holz- und Bohrwürmer geschützt. Um Wärmeaufladungen, die in den Stahlbetonkonstruktionen Wärmespannungen erzeugen, möglichst zu vermeiden, sind Baustoffe mit geringem Wärmespeichervermögen und schattenspendende Konstruktionen vorgesehen worden. Tragende Stahlkonstruktionen kamen grundsätzlich nicht zur Ausführung, da diese trotz Rostschutzanstrich wegen der in Tema herrschenden hohen relativen Luftfeuchtigkeit (95 bis 100 Prozent, mittags sinkt sie auf etwa 60 bis 70 Prozent ab) und der salzhaltigen Luft der Korrosionsgefahr ausgesetzt sind.

Um für gewisse Bauabschnitte (gedeckte Übergänge, offene Wagenunterstellplätze, Werkeinzäunung) einen Vorlauf für die Bauausführung zu schaffen, wurden Stahlbetonfertigteile entwickelt, die auf der Baustelle durch den Baubetrieb vorgefertigt wurden.

Bauausführung

Das Bauobjekt „Regierungsdruckerei Tema in Ghana" umfaßte die Teilobjekte:
Geländeplanierung,
Versorgungsleitungen,
Be- und Entwässerung sowie Straßenbau,
Produktionsgebäude (Schiffe I – V),
Trafostation,
Redaktions- und Verwaltungsgebäude,
Speisesaal (Mehrzweckssaal) und Küche,
WC-, Wasch- und Umkleideräume,
Werkgaragen,
Kraftwagenunterstellräume mit Pförtnergebäude,
Werkeinzäunung, Terrassen- und Brüstungsmauern,
überdeckte Gänge.

541

Bauausführung

Das Bauobjekt „Regierungsdruckerei Tema in Ghana" umfasste die Teilobjekte:

Geländeplanierung,
Versorgungsleitungen,
Be- und Entwässerung sowie Straßenbau,
Produktionsgebäude (Schiffe I–IV)
Trafostation
Redaktions- und Verwaltungsgebäude,
Speisesaal (Mehrzwecksaal) und Küche,
WC-, Wasch und Umkleideräume,
Werkgaragen,
Kraftwagenunterstellräume mit Pförtnergebäude,
Werkeinzäunung, Terrassen- und Brüstungsmauern,
überdeckte Gänge.

the government printing press was to be a highlight of this area from an architectural and urbanist perspective. The choice was also made on the basis of infrastructural and transport considerations. The site is located to the west of road no. 36 and is to be bordered to the west by the ring road that is currently being planned. It slopes very steeply from southeast to northwest. The access roads were positioned on road no. 36.

CONCEPT AND DESIGN

It has long been the case in the printing industry that compact construction is the system of building that is most effective in terms of both economic performance and the overall functionality of the technology. Even in the tropics, this can be realized in particular circumstances. The climatic conditions here necessitate good natural cross ventilation in all the rooms, since it would be uneconomical to provide central ventilation or even air conditioning systems in the production halls. Local air-conditioning units or ventilation systems have only been put in some of the sections of the five-aisled production halls. In order to prevent direct insolation from “heating up” the interior of the production building, it had to be oriented along the east–west longitudinal axis, as the strongest solar radiation comes from the east and west. The southern position of the sun is not a concern as it is vertical at the zenith. The main wind direction is crucial to ensuring the natural ventilation of the building, and the windows needed to be arranged accordingly.

The heavy downpours during the rainy season require carefully designed roof structures with large overhangs. The wind direction and the main direction of the rain were decisive factors here. This gave rise to the unconventional appearance of the roof shapes in various buildings.

Based on the requirements defined by the chief engineer, excellent natural lighting conditions were to be created for the hall bays of the production building. The orientation of the large louver windows had to be north-northeast to guarantee continuous daylight throughout the day.

The roofs of the production building are provided with sound-absorbing suspended ceilings and ventilated accordingly. A thermal insulation material,

städtebaulichen und architektonischen Akzent für dieses Gebiet darstellen sollte. Außerdem war die Standortwahl auch von versorgungs- und verkehrstechnischen Überlegungen abhängig gemacht worden.

Das Baugelände liegt westlich der Straße Nr. 36 und soll westlich von der in der Planung befindlichen Auto-Ringstraße begrenzt werden. Es fällt sehr stark von Südost nach Nordwest ab. Die Zufahrten waren an der Straße Nr. 36 anzuordnen.

ENTWURF UND GESTALTUNG

Seit langem schon ist für die grafische Industrie der Kompaktbau die bauliche Anlage, die für die Gesamtfunktion der Technologie ausgezeichnete ökonomische Ergebnisse bringt. Auch in den Tropen ist der Kompaktbau unter besonderen Bedingungen realisierbar. Die klimatischen Verhältnisse der Tropen verlangen eine sehr gute natürliche Querlüftung aller Räume des Kompaktbaus, da es unökonomisch wäre, für die Produktionshallen zentrale Lüftungs- oder gar Klimaanlagen vorzusehen. Lediglich in verschiedenen Abteilungen der Produktion sind örtliche Klimageräte (Airconditions) oder örtliche Be- und Entlüftungsanlagen in der fünfschiffigen Produktionshalle angeordnet worden. Um eine „Aufheizung“ im Innern des Produktionsgebäudes durch direkte Sonneneinstrahlung zu verhindern, mußte das Gebäude in der Längsachse Ost-West orientiert werden, da die stärkste Sonneneinstrahlung von Osten und Westen erfolgt. Der südliche Sonnenstand ist unproblematisch, da dieser senkrecht ist. Für die natürliche Durchlüftung der Gebäude ist die Hauptwindrichtung maßgebend, das heißt, die Fensteranordnung mußte sich danach richten.

Die in der Regenzeit einsetzenden sehr starken Regengüsse verlangen wohlüberlegte Dachkonstruktionen mit großen Dachüberständen. Die Windrichtung und die Hauptregenrichtung waren dabei mitbestimmende Faktoren. Dadurch entstanden die eigenwillig anmutenden Dachformen bei verschiedenen Gebäuden.

Für die Hallenschiffe des Produktionsgebäudes sollten nach der Aufgabenstellung des Generalprojektanten sehr gute natürliche Lichtverhältnisse geschaffen werden. Die Orientierung der großen Louvres-Fenster mußte nach Nord-Nordost erfolgen, um ein den ganzen Tag über kontinuierliches Tageslicht zu garantieren.

4. General view of the printing facility from the south-west
5. Partial view from the east
6. The production halls under construction, 1:1000
7. View from east, 1:1000
9. Cross section through the production hall, 1:200

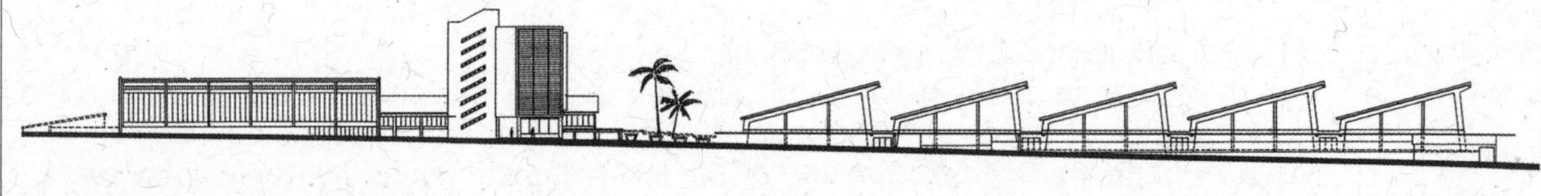

7

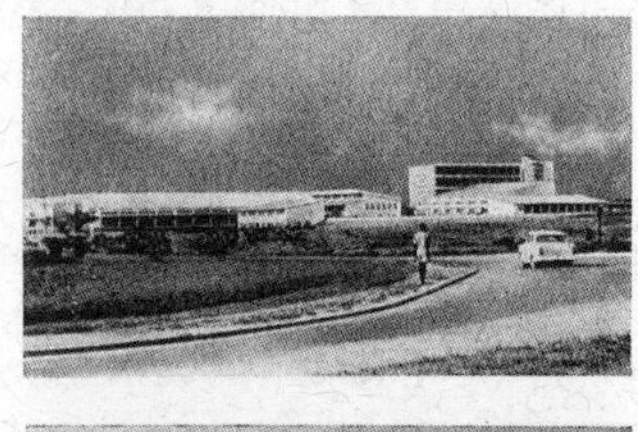

4

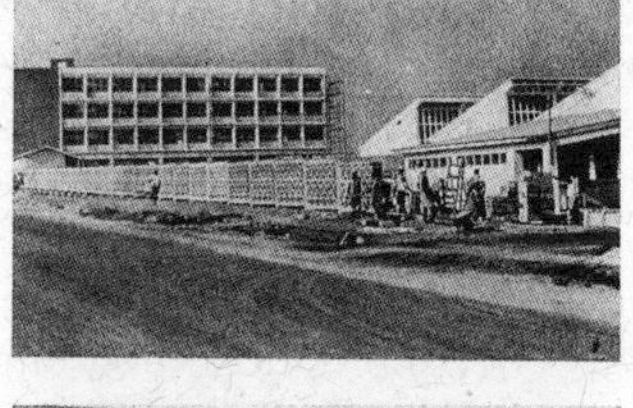

5

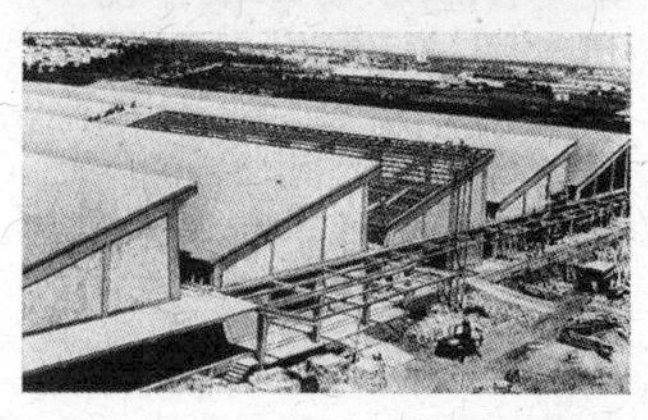

6

Außerdem wurde dem Auftraggeber ein Vorschlag für die grünplanerische Lösung des Industriegeländes unterbreitet. Es muß hier gesagt werden, daß der Auftraggeber von Anfang an Klarheit über diese Aufgabe besaß und daß die der Projektierung vorausgegangene Studie sehr schnell von ihm bestätigt wurde.

Da dieses Objekt von der Regierung Ghanas geplant war, stand der Realisierung der Maßnahme ab Juni 1962 nichts im Wege, zumal die Projektanten keinen Verzug in der Auslieferung der Teilobjektunterlagen verursachten. So war es möglich, zügig den Baustellenaufschluß und die Grobplanierungsarbeiten durchzuführen. Die Gründungsarbeiten für die Teilobjekte und die Herstellung der monolithischen Stahlbetonkonstruktionen wurden von mehreren hundert ghanesischen Arbeitern ausgeführt. Die Materialversorgung lief kontinuierlich und war abgestimmt mit den erforderlichen Zwischenterminen. Durch den Einsatz von zwei deutschen Bauleitern auf der Baustelle (Konsultanten) war es immer möglich, schnelle Entscheidungen zwischen Generalprojektanten und Baufirma herbeizuführen. Da die Baufirma das Gesamtobjekt pauschal nach der von ihr ermittelten Kostenangebotssumme übernommen hatte, waren Änderungen gegenüber den Projektunterlagen durch Variation-Order (Änderungs-Protokoll) zu belegen. Dem guten Zusammenwirken der Verantwortlichen der Baufirma und der deutschen Fachleute ist es zu verdanken, daß die gestellten Zwischentermine für Rohbaufertigstellung und Freigabe für die Ausrüstungsmontage eingehalten wurden.

Der Verfasser des Berichtes konnte sich über den Stand der Bauarbeiten im April dieses Jahres bei der Wahrnehmung der bautechnischen Autorenkontrolle orientieren und kommt schlußfolgernd zu dem Ergebnis, daß in der Hafenstadt Tema ein Bauwerk entsteht, das den gestellten Anforderungen gerecht wird.

Die Bauausführung ist als sehr gut zu bewerten. Man kann den ghanesischen Arbeitern aller Gewerke und auch den leitenden Ingenieuren der Baufirma für ihre Leistungen nur höchste Anerkennung zollen. Es kann eingeschätzt werden, daß das Zusammenwirken aller an diesem Projekt verantwortlichen Institutionen Ghanas und der DDR in der Projektierung und Ausführung vorbildlich war.

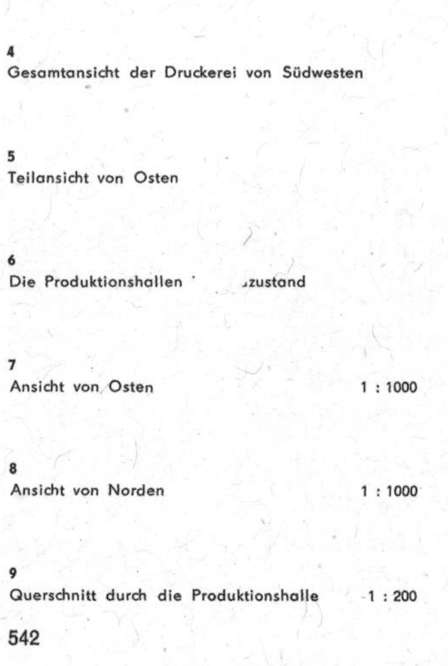

4
Gesamtansicht der Druckerei von Südwesten

5
Teilansicht von Osten

6
Die Produktionshallen ... zustand

7
Ansicht von Osten 1 : 1000

8
Ansicht von Norden 1 : 1000

9
Querschnitt durch die Produktionshalle 1 : 200

542

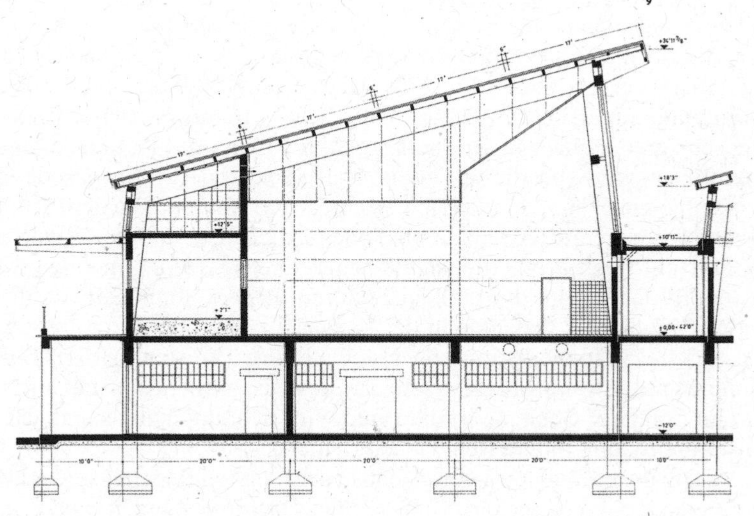

9

4. Gesamtansicht der Druckerei von Südwesten
5. Teilansicht von Osten
6. Die Produktionshallen im Bauzustand
7. Ansicht von Osten 1 : 1000
8. Ansicht von Norden 1 : 1000
9. Querschnitt durch die Produktionshalle 1 : 200

which is arranged under the upper roof skin (corrugated aluminum), has the additional function of reducing the drum effect when it rains. Measurements of the temperatures inside the building have been on average 5–6°C lower than outside the halls. This has been achieved by implementing the planned roof construction in conjunction with the building ventilation.

CONSTRUCTION

The monolithic reinforced concrete frame construction is preferred in Ghana. It must meet the requirements set out in the West African Building Regulations. The wall infills are made with concrete blocks or hollow concrete stones. The foundations were laid on weathered gneissic rock and geared to the provisions laid down for earthquake areas, which are listed in the building regulations. It is customary in the country for the structural elements supporting the roof to be made of mahogany wood. The wood used in the building, which has a load-bearing function, is protected against termites, woodworm, and bore worms. In order to avoid as much as possible the heat buildup that creates thermal stresses in the reinforced concrete structures, building materials with low heat-storage capacity and shade-giving structures were used. Load-bearing steel structures were generally not used, as they are exposed to the risk of corrosion—even when a rust-protection coating is applied—owing to the high humidity prevailing in Tema (95–100 percent, which at noon drops to around 60–70 percent) and the salty air.

Precast reinforced concrete elements were developed to expedite the construction work on certain sections (covered walkways, open parking spaces, fencing). These were prefabricated on-site by the construction company.

In addition, a proposal for the landscape master plan of the industrial site was submitted to the contracting authority, who, it should be said, had a clear sense of the task at hand from the beginning, and the study preceding the project planning was confirmed by them very quickly.

With the Ghanaian government as the project planner, implementation could proceed unimpeded from June 1962 onwards, particularly as the sub-project

Die Dächer des Produktionsgebäudes sind mit schallschluckenden, abgehängten Zwischendecken versehen und entsprechend durchlüftet. Ein Wärmedämmstoff, der unter der oberen Dachhaut (Wellaluminium) angeordnet ist, hat außerdem die Funktion, die Trommelwirkung bei Regen zu mindern. Im Gebäudeinnern sind im Mittel 5–6°C niedrigere Temperaturen gemessen worden als außerhalb der Hallen. Dies ist durch die vorgesehene Dachkonstruktion im Zusammenspiel mit der Gebäudelüftung erreicht worden.

KONSTRUKTION

Der monolithische Stahlbetonskelettbau wird in Ghana bevorzugt. Er muß den Forderungen, die in den „Westafrikanischen Baubestimmungen" festgelegt sind, entsprechen. Die Wandausfachungen werden mit Betonblöcken oder Betonhohlsteinen ausgeführt. Die Fundamentierung erfolgte auf verwittertem Gneis und richtete sich nach den für Erdbebengebiete festgelegten Bestimmungen, die in der obenangeführten Bauordnung enthalten sind. Es ist landesüblich, daß die dachhauttragenden Konstruktionselemente aus Mahagoniholz vorgesehen werden. Das im Bauwerk verwendete Holz, das tragende Funktionen übernehmen muß, wird gegen Termiten, Holz- und Bohrwürmer geschützt. Um Wärmeaufladungen, die in der Stahlbetonkonstruktionen Wärmespannungen erzeugen, möglichst zu vermeiden, sind Baustoffe mit geringem Wärmespeichervermögen und schattenspendende Konstruktionen vorgesehen worden. Tragende Stahlkonstruktionen kamen grundsätzlich nicht zur Ausführung, da diese trotz Rostschutzanstrich wegen der in Tema herrschenden hohen Luftfeuchtigkeit (95 bis 100 Prozent, mittags sinkt sie auf etwa 60 bis 70 Prozent ab) und der salzhaltigen Luft der Korrosionsgefahr ausgesetzt sind.

Um für gewisse Bauabschnitte (gedeckte Übergänge, offene Wagenunterstellplätze, Werkeinzäunung) einen Vorlauf für die Bauausführung zu schaffen, wurden Stahlbetonfertigteile entwickelt, die auf der Baustelle durch Baubetrieb vorgefertigt wurden.

Außerdem wurde dem Auftraggeber ein Vorschlag für die grünplanerische Lösung des Industriegeländes unterbreitet. Es muß hier gesagt werden, daß der Auftraggeber von Anfang an Klarheit über diese Aufgabe besaß und daß die der Projektierung vorausgegangene Studie sehr schnell von ihm bestätigt wurde.

Ground floor, 1:1000

1 Manual typesetting
2 Intertype department
3 Corrections
4 Monotype buttons
5 Monotype caster
6 Stereotype / electroplating
7 Darkroom
8 Chemigraphy
9 Copying
10 Silver syringes
11 Clichographs
12 Finishing hall / press proof
13 Head of department
14 Letterpress/sheet-fed printing
15 Printing plate preparation
16 Exercise book production
17 Rotation department
18 Circular stereotype
19 Head of department
20 Darkroom
21 Photography
22 Retouching
23 Copying machine
24 Frame copy
25 Preparation
26 Finishing
27 Assembly
28 Press proof
29 Small-format offset presses
30 Large-format offset presses
31 Book block processing
32 Further processing of small print products
33 Single-sheet processing
34 Head of department
35 Paper warehouse

Basement, 1:1000

1 Mechanical workshop
2 Plate-grinding shop
3 Spare parts storage
4 Electrical workshop
5 Roller storage
6 Compressor room
7 Extra space
8 Material storage
9 Color storage
10 Chemical storage
11 Film storage
12 Typesetting storage
13 Finished goods storage
14 Wastepaper storage
15 Wastepaper storage, discharge chamber
16 Wastepaper storage, low-pressure chamber
17 Finished goods storage
18 Ventilator room
19 Canvassing shop
20 Cardboard storage
21 Adhesive preparation
A Ventilation ducts
B Cable ducts
C Backfilled rooms

Erdgeschoß 1 : 1000

1 Handsatz
2 Intertype-Abteilung
3 Korrektoren
4 Monotype-Taster
5 Monotype-Gießer
6 Stereotypie – Galvanoplastik
7 Dunkelkammer
8 Chemigrafie
9 Kopie
10 Silberspritzen
11 Klischografen
12 Fertigmacherei – Andruck
13 Abteilungsleiter
14 Buchdruck / Bogendruck
15 Druckformenvorbereitung
16 Schulheftherstellung
17 Rotationsabteilung
18 Rundstereotypie
19 Abteilungsleiter
20 Dunkelkammer
21 Fotografie
22 Retusche
23 Kopiermaschine
24 Rahmenkopie
25 Präparation
26 Fertigmachen
27 Montage
28 Andruck
29 Kleinformatige Offsetmaschinen
30 Großformatige Offsetmaschinen
31 Buchblockverarbeitung
32 Weiterverarbeitung von Kleindrucksachen
33 Einzelbogenbearbeitung
34 Abteilungsleiter
35 Papierlager

Sockelgeschoß 1 : 1000

1 Mechanische Werkstatt
2 Plattenschleiferei
3 Ersatzteillager
4 Elektrowerkstatt
5 Walzenlager
6 Kompressorraum
7 Reserveraum
8 Materiallager
9 Farblager
10 Chemikalienlager
11 Filmlager
12 Satzlager
13 Fertigwarenlager
14 Altpapierlager
15 Altpapier-Abwurfkammer
16 Altpapier-Unterdruckkamer
17 Fertigwarenlager
18 Ventilatorraum
19 Deckenmacherei
20 Pappenlager
21 Klebstoffvorbereitung
A Belüftungskanäle
B Kabelkanäle
C Hinterfüllte Räume

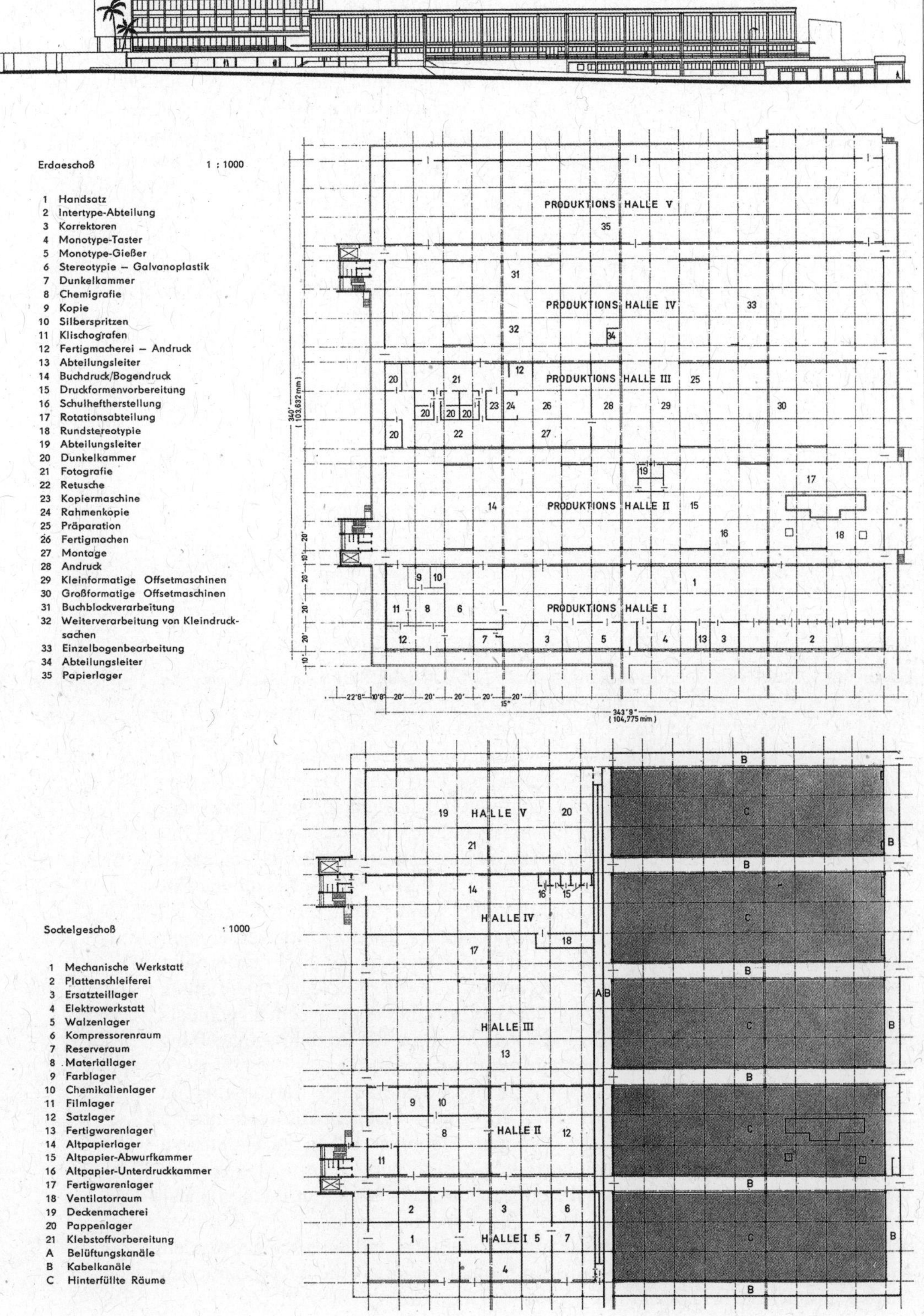

Erdaeschoß 1 : 1000

1 Handsatz
2 Intertype-Abteilung
3 Korrektoren
4 Monotype-Taster
5 Monotype-Gießer
6 Stereotypie – Galvanoplastik
7 Dunkelkammer
8 Chemigrafie
9 Kopie
10 Silberspritzen
11 Klischografen
12 Fertigmacherei – Andruck
13 Abteilungsleiter
14 Buchdruck/Bogendruck
15 Druckformenvorbereitung
16 Schulheftherstellung
17 Rotationsabteilung
18 Rundstereotypie
19 Abteilungsleiter
20 Dunkelkammer
21 Fotografie
22 Retusche
23 Kopiermaschine
24 Rahmenkopie
25 Präparation
26 Fertigmachen
27 Montage
28 Andruck
29 Kleinformatige Offsetmaschinen
30 Großformatige Offsetmaschinen
31 Buchblockverarbeitung
32 Weiterverarbeitung von Kleindrucksachen
33 Einzelbogenbearbeitung
34 Abteilungsleiter
35 Papierlager

Sockelgeschoß 1 : 1000

1 Mechanische Werkstatt
2 Plattenschleiferei
3 Ersatzteillager
4 Elektrowerkstatt
5 Walzenlager
6 Kompressorenraum
7 Reserveraum
8 Materiallager
9 Farblager
10 Chemikalienlager
11 Filmlager
12 Satzlager
13 Fertigwarenlager
14 Altpapierlager
15 Altpapier-Abwurfkammer
16 Altpapier-Unterdruckkammer
17 Fertigwarenlager
18 Ventilatorraum
19 Deckenmacherei
20 Pappenlager
21 Klebstoffvorbereitung
A Belüftungskanäle
B Kabelkanäle
C Hinterfüllte Räume

documentation was delivered promptly. Thus, it was possible to carry out the site development and rough grading work expeditiously. The foundation work for the sub-projects and the construction of the monolithic reinforced concrete structures were executed by several hundred Ghanaian workers. There was a continuous supply of materials, and this was coordinated with the required interim deadlines. Two German construction supervisors were deployed on the construction site (consultants), which meant that it was always possible for the general project planners and the construction company to make quick decisions together. As the construction company had taken on the entire project for a fixed fee based on the costings calculated in their proposal, changes to the project documentation had to be verified by means of variation orders. The excellent cooperation between those responsible at the construction company and the German specialists ensured that all the interim deadlines for completing the building shell were met and the equipment installation was approved as per the schedule.

The author of this report assessed the status of the construction work in April of this year during the technical inspection and has concluded that the structure being built in the port city of Tema meets all the specified requirements.

The execution of the construction project can be evaluated as very good. The Ghanaian workers in all trades and the leading engineers in the construction company deserve great credit for their achievements. The cooperation between all the responsible institutions in Ghana and East Germany proved exemplary in terms of both planning and realization.

Da dieses Objekt von der Regierung Ghanas geplant war, stand der Realisierung der Maßnahme ab Juni 1962 nichts im Wege, zumal die Projektanten keinen Verzug in der Auslieferung der Teilobjektunterlagen verursachten. So war es möglich, zügig den Baustellenaufschluß und die Grobplanierungsarbeiten durchzuführen. Die Gründungsarbeiten für die Teilobjekte und die Herstellung der monolithischen Stahlbetonkonstruktionen wurden von mehreren hundert ghanesischen Arbeitern ausgeführt. Die Materialversorgung lief kontinuierlich und war abgestimmt mit den erforderlichen Zwischenterminen. Durch den Einsatz von zwei deutschen Bauleitern auf der Baustelle (Konsultanten) war es immer möglich, schnelle Entscheidungen zwischen Generalprojektanten und Baufirma herbeizuführen. Da die Baufirma das Gesamtobjekt pauschal nach der von ihr ermittelten Kostenangebotssumme übernommen hatte, waren Änderungen gegenüber den Projektunterlagen durch Variation-Order (Änderungsprotokoll) zu belegen. Dem guten Zusammenwirken der Verantwortlichen der Baufirma und der deutschen Fachleute ist es zu verdanken, daß die gestellten Zwischentermine für Rohbaufertigstellung und Freigabe für die Ausrüstungsmontage eingehalten wurden.

Der Verfasser des Berichtes konnte sich über den Stand der Bauarbeiten im April dieses Jahres bei der Wahrnehmung der bautechnischen Autorenkontrolle orientieren und kommt schlußfolgernd zu dem Ergebnis, daß in der Hafenstadt Tema ein Bauwerk entsteht, das den gestellten Anforderungen gerecht wird.

Die Bauausführung ist als sehr gut zu bewerten. Man kann den ghanesischen Arbeitern aller Gewerke und auch den leitenden Ingenieuren der Baufirma für ihre Leistungen nur höchste Anerkennung zollen. Es kann eingeschätzt werden, daß das Zusammenwirken aller an diesem Projekt verantwortlichen Institutionen Ghanas und der DDR in der Projektierung und Ausführung vorbildlich war.

CONVERSATION WITH ROGER BEKOE-DAWSON

Ato Annan

GESPRÄCH MIT ROGER BEKOE-DAWSON

This conversation was conducted by Ato Annan on May 27, 2021. The interview has been edited from its original audio version for the sake of clarity.

In this conversation, artist and curator Ato Annan speaks with Roger Bekoe-Dawson, former head of Ghana Publishing and the government printing house. The two reflect on the legacy of the Tema Printing Press—one of the most modern printing facilities in West Africa, it was completed in 1964 during Kwame Nkrumah's presidency with the support of the German Democratic Republic (GDR). Bekoe-Dawson shares insights into Ghana's state publishing history, recounts his personal stories from his time working there, and explains how political shifts and privatization policies eventually led to the decline of these state institutions.

Mr. Bekoe-Dawson, I appreciate your taking the time to have this conversation with me. Could you tell us a bit about your association with the Tema Printing Press?

From 1965 to 1967, I worked in the administrative department of the press—that was just a year after it had been completed and commissioned. It was one of the most modern factories at the time. I say factories because there were others around, like Lever Brothers. The printing house in Tema was quite unique—it was the only facility at the time that had buses transporting workers from various areas to work. We also had some German trainers. I left in 1967.

You left after just two years of working there?

Yes, I left to further my studies after gaining admission to the Kwame Nkrumah University of Science and Technology (KNUST), where I chose to study graphics. Because of my earlier experience at the Tema Printing Press, I always returned there for internships whenever the opportunity came up—so in a way, I maintained a long-standing connection with the press. After graduating, I worked in advertising for a while, then went on to pursue a six-year program in medical illustration at the University of Maiduguri in Nigeria. When I returned, I rejoined the press in Tema. At that time, the management of Ghana Publishing had been dissolved, and I was appointed chairman of the new management committee. I was later made managing

Dieses Gespräch wurde von Ato Annan am 27. Mai 2021 geführt. Das Interview wurde aus Gründen der Lesbarkeit gegenüber der Original-Audioaufnahme redaktionell bearbeitet.

In diesem Gespräch trifft der Künstler und Kurator Ato Annan auf Roger Bekoe-Dawson, den ehemaligen Leiter von Ghana Publishing und der Regierungsdruckerei. Die beiden diskutieren über das Vermächtnis der Tema Printing Press – einer der modernsten Druckereien Westafrikas, die 1964 während der Präsidentschaft von Kwame Nkrumah mit Unterstützung der Deutschen Demokratischen Republik (DDR) fertiggestellt wurde. Bekoe-Dawson gibt Einblicke in die Geschichte des staatlichen Verlagswesens in Ghana, erzählt persönliche Geschichten aus seiner Zeit und berichtet, wie politische Veränderungen und Privatisierungsmaßnahmen schließlich zum Niedergang dieser staatlichen Institutionen führten.

Herr Roger Bekoe-Dawson, vielen Dank, dass Sie sich Zeit für dieses Gespräch genommen haben. Können Sie uns etwas über Ihre Verbindung zur Tema Printing Press erzählen?

Von 1965 bis 1967 habe ich in der Verwaltung der Druckerei gearbeitet, ich bin also bereits ein Jahr nach ihrer Fertigstellung und Inbetriebnahme dort eingestiegen. Sie gehörte zu den modernsten Fabriken ihrer Zeit. Ich sage Fabriken, denn es gab noch einige andere in der Umgebung, zum Beispiel Lever Brothers. Die Druckerei in Tema war ziemlich einzigartig. Sie war damals das einzige Unternehmen, das über Busse verfügte, um Arbeiter·innen aus verschiedenen Gegenden zur Arbeit zu bringen. Wir hatten auch einige deutsche Ausbilder·innen. 1967 habe ich gekündigt.

Sie sind also nur zwei Jahre geblieben?

Ja, ich habe mein Studium fortgesetzt, sobald ich an der Kwame Nkrumah University of Science and Technology (KNUST) angenommen war, wo ich mich für Grafikdesign eingeschrieben habe. Aufgrund meiner früheren Erfahrungen bei der Tema Printing Press bin ich für Praktika dorthin zurückgekehrt, wann immer sich die Gelegenheit bot. So habe ich über viele Jahre eine Verbindung zur Druckerei aufrechterhalten. Nach meinem Abschluss arbeitete ich lange in der Werbebranche und absolvierte anschließend ein sechsjähriges Studium der medizinischen Illustration an der Universität von Maiduguri in Nigeria. Nach meiner Rückkehr landete ich wieder bei der Druckerei in Tema. Zu dieser Zeit war die Geschäftsführung von

director—essentially, the Government Printer, if you want to call it that. I served in that role from 1990 until I resigned in 2003. The Tema Printing Press was quite unique—that was Nkrumah's own concept. It had additional facilities as well, including a laundry. Everything was well structured at the time. Nkrumah's vision was to make it the government's primary printing facility—so much so that, had things gone as planned and had he remained in power, it could even have printed currency. It's a shame the place has been demolished. The area across the road, where you now find cold stores and other businesses, was originally intended to be a printing village—a hub for producing textbooks and other educational materials, even for other African countries. That was Nkrumah's vision for Ghana Publishing.

We are talking specifically about the Tema Press, but it's important to understand that within the government structure, Ghana Publishing had four main divisions. One of these was Sales and Distribution, which was responsible for distributing free textbooks—a key part of Nkrumah's vision. At the time, everything related to textbooks—publishing, printing, and distribution—was coordinated within this system. The *My First Copy Book* I had, like those of many others then, came directly from this

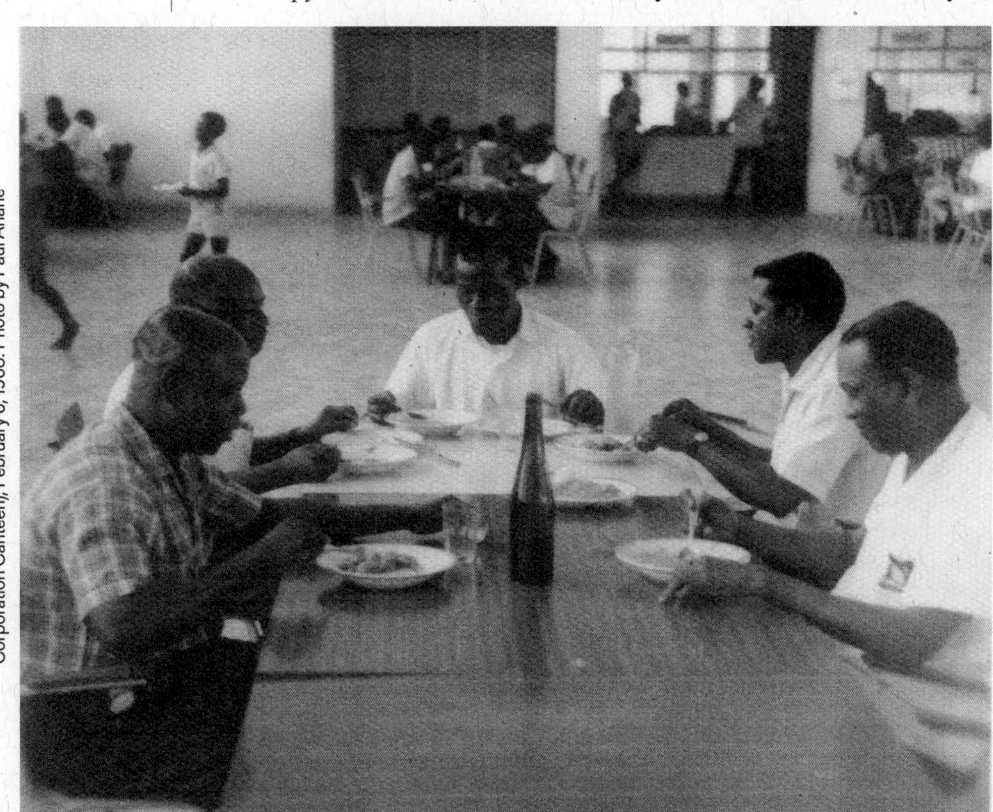

Tema in twenty-four hours (State Publishing Corporation Canteen), February 6, 1968. Photo by Paul Anane

Tema in 24 Stunden (Kantine der Staatlichen Verlagsgesellschaft), 6. Februar 1968. Foto von Paul Anane

Ghana Publishing aufgelöst worden, und ich wurde Vorsitzender des neuen Verwaltungsausschusses. Später wurde ich zum Geschäftsführer ernannt – zum Regierungsdrucker, wenn man so will. Diese Funktion hatte ich von 1990 bis zu meinem Ausscheiden im Jahr 2003 inne. Die Tema Printing Press war außergewöhnlich. Sie war Nkrumahs eigene Idee. Sie verfügte auch über zusätzliche Einrichtungen, darunter eine Wäscherei. Damals war alles gut strukturiert. Nkrumahs Vision war es, sie zur Hauptdruckerei der Regierung zu machen. So dass sie, wenn alles nach Plan verlaufen und er an der Macht geblieben wäre, sogar Geld hätte drucken können. Es ist schade, dass alles abgerissen wurde. Das Gebiet auf der anderen Straßenseite, wo sich heute Kühlhäuser und andere Unternehmen befinden, sollte ursprünglich ein Druckereidorf werden – ein Zentrum für die Produktion von Lehrbüchern und weiteren Bildungsmaterialien, sogar für andere afrikanische Länder. Das war Nkrumahs Vision für Ghana Publishing.

Wir sprechen hier speziell über die Tema Press, aber es ist wichtig zu verstehen, dass Ghana Publishing als Staatsunternehmen vier Hauptabteilungen hatte. Eine davon war der Vertrieb, der für die Verteilung kostenloser Schulbücher zuständig war – ein wichtiger Teil von Nkrumahs Vision. Damals wurde alles, was mit Schulbüchern zu tun hatte – Veröffentlichung, Druck und Vertrieb – innerhalb dieses Systems koordiniert.

1. *My First Copy Book* is a popular activity book for preschoolers, kindergartens, and primary school learners in Ghana to enhance writing and lettering skills.

publishing outfit.[1] So, when we talk about publishing in that era, it wasn't just a matter of printing books, it was a comprehensive operation that involved publishing, printing, and distributing educational materials—mainly textbooks. All of this work was intended to be carried out specifically at the Tema Printing Press, within the purview of the printing division. The Sales and Distribution division managed the free textbook distribution, while other aspects were overseen by the Publishing and Distribution divisions.

The Victoriaborg Printing Press also existed as a government printer, responsible for printing all stationery for government offices in Ghana. It also handled the printing of receipt books, vouchers, and especially parliamentary documents such as Hansards. However, it was originally built by the British colonial government. The Assembly Press, which is now the only existing government printer, was part of the Victoriaborg facility. There was another government printer in Takoradi around Monkey Hill which was also responsible for the printing of railway tickets and market tickets, but I think was it was also sold as part of the program of state divestiture. At that time, printing for the government was centralized and handled by various government printers. Everything related to government documents was printed based on the type of material. Depending on what needed to be printed, it would be sent to the Tema Printing Press, Assembly Press, Takoradi Printing Press, or Tamale Printing Press. Tema Press was solely responsible for distributing the textbooks it printed, which is why we had facilities in all the regions. We even had estate houses—for instance, in Kumasi, though some of those were later sold off. There were similar setups in places like Sunyani too. All of that was to support textbook distribution.

Let me take you back a bit to retrace the trajectory of the Tema Printing Press—from its completion in 1964 and the start of operations to when you joined in 1965. At the time, it was printing and distributing

Wie so viele andere auch hatte ich *First Copy Books*, die direkt aus diesem Verlag stammten.[1] Wenn wir also über das Verlagswesen in dieser Zeit sprechen, ging es nicht nur um den Druck von Büchern, sondern um einen verzweigten Betrieb, der die Veröffentlichung, den Druck und den Vertrieb von Bildungsmaterialien – hauptsächlich Schulbüchern – umfasste. All diese Arbeiten sollten speziell in der Tema Printing Press, der Druckabteilung, durchgeführt werden. Die Vertriebsabteilung war für die kostenlose Verteilung der Lehrbücher zuständig, während andere Aspekte von den Abteilungen Verlag und Vertrieb überwacht wurden.

Die Victoriaborg Printing Press war ebenfalls eine staatliche Druckerei, die für den Druck aller Schreibwaren für Regierungsbehörden in Ghana zuständig war. Sie übernahm auch den Druck von Quittungsbüchern, Belegen und insbesondere von Parlamentsdokumenten wie den Hansards, also den Parlamentsprotokollen. Sie wurde jedoch ursprünglich von der britischen Kolonialregierung erbaut. Die Assembly Press, die einzige heute noch existierende staatliche Druckerei, war Teil der Victoriaborg-Anlage. Es gab noch eine weitere staatliche Druckerei in Takoradi, in der Nähe des Monkey-Hill-Walds. Sie war unter anderem für den Druck von Eisenbahnfahrkarten und Marktkarten zuständig. Aber ich glaube, sie wurde ebenfalls verkauft. Zu dieser Zeit war der Druck für die Regierung zentralisiert und wurde von verschiedenen staatlichen Druckereien übernommen. Abhängig vom Material, wurden dann die offiziellen Dokumente an verschiedenen Orten hergestellt. Je nachdem, was gedruckt werden musste, wurde es entweder an die Tema Printing Press, die Assembly Press, die Takoradi Printing Press oder die Tamale Printing Press geschickt. Die Tema Printing Press war allein für den Vertrieb der von ihr gedruckten Schulbücher verantwortlich, weshalb wir in allen Regionen über Zweigstellen verfügten. Wir hatten sogar Anwesen, zum Beispiel in Kumasi, von denen einige später verkauft wurden. Ähnliche Einrichtungen gab es auch an Orten wie Sunyani. All dies diente der Unterstützung der Lehrbuchverteilung.

Lassen Sie uns etwas genauer auf den Werdegang der Tema Printing Press blicken – seit ihrer Fertigstellung im Jahr 1964 und der Aufnahme

1. *My First Copy Book* ist ein beliebtes Buch für Kindergartenkinder, Vor- und Grundschüler·innen zur Verbesserung der Schreibfähigkeiten.

educational materials across the country, supported by Nkrumah's strong interest in the initiative. But then, in 1966, Nkrumah was overthrown. What happened to the Tema Printing Press after that?

After Nkrumah was overthrown in 1966, most of what he started came under attack and was vilified. Things didn't follow the original plan anymore. Then private printers started showing up and competing seriously with Ghana Publishing. Honestly, back then, people often went with the private printers, even when the work was supposed to go to Ghana Publishing. The government printer had to compete directly with private printing firms, who could easily undercut prices, offer incentives, and pay tips. As a result, Ghana Publishing began losing its footing and gradually saw its share of the market decline.

And what period are we talking about here—would this have been in the '70s or '80s?

It was a gradual process, continuing until I became the managing director in the '90s.

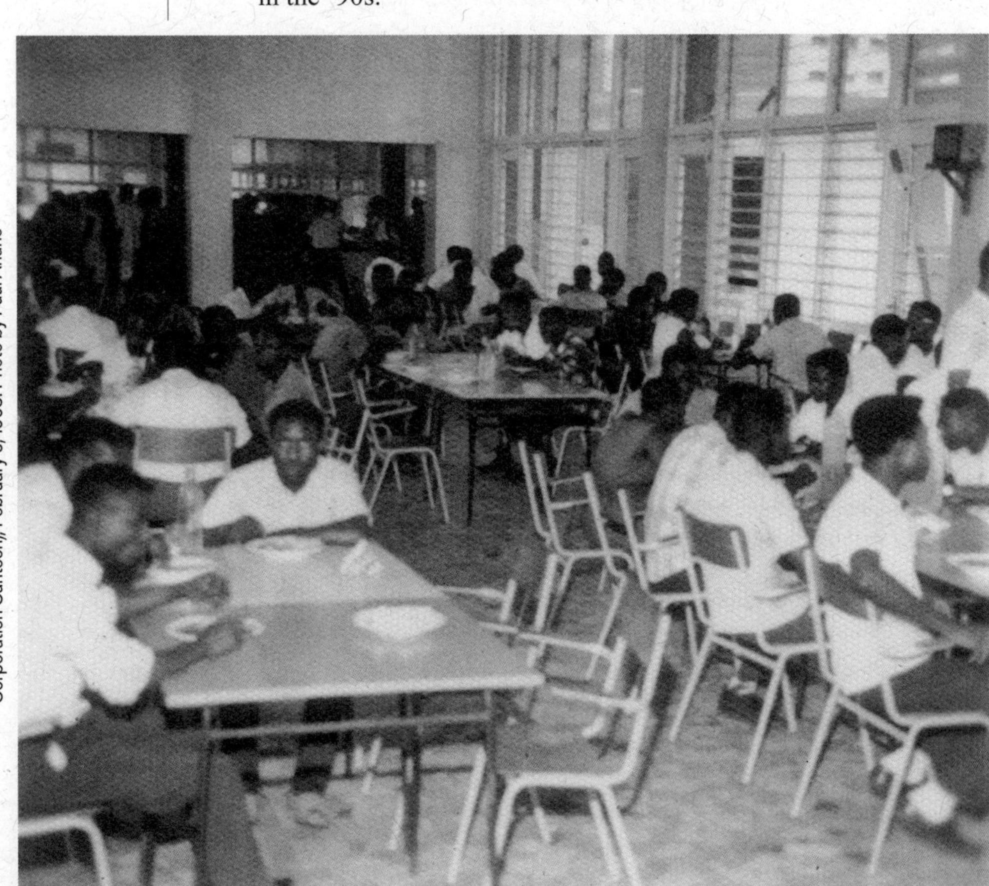

Tema in twenty-four hours (State Publishing Corporation Canteen), February 6, 1968. Photo by Paul Anane

Tema in 24 Stunden (Kantine der Staatlichen Verlagsgesellschaft), 6. Februar 1968. Foto von Paul Anane

des Betriebs und Ihrem Eintritt im Jahr 1965. Damals druckte und vertrieb sie Bildungsmaterialien im ganzen Land. Nkrumah hatte großes Interesse an dieser Initiative. Im Jahr 1966 wurde Nkrumah jedoch gestürzt. Was geschah danach mit der Tema Printing Press?

Nach dem Sturz Nkrumahs 1966 wurde fast alles, was er begonnen hatte, angegriffen und diffamiert. Die Dinge verliefen nicht mehr nach dem ursprünglichen Plan. Es tauchten private Druckereien auf und machten Ghana Publishing ernsthafte Konkurrenz. Die Leute gingen damals oft zu den privaten Druckereien, auch wenn die Aufträge eigentlich an Ghana Publishing hätten gehen sollen. Die staatliche Druckerei musste direkt mit privaten Druckereien konkurrieren, die leicht Preise unterbieten, Anreize schaffen und Unterstützung anbieten konnten. Infolgedessen verlor Ghana Publishing – die staatliche Druckerei – an Boden und musste einen allmählichen Verlust von Marktanteilen hinnehmen.

Von welchem Zeitraum sprechen wir dabei? War das in den 1970er oder 80er Jahren?

Es war ein schrittweiser Prozess, der sich bis zu meiner Ernennung zum Geschäftsführer in den 90er Jahren fortsetzte.

I suppose, as a government entity, you had to follow official channels and adhere to proper procedures.

Yes, but when you're up against private companies the situation changes. They could offer perks, like inviting you to lunch or even arranging a trip abroad or to their home. How could we possibly compete with that? These were some of the challenges we faced. But let's return to the Tema Printing Press. You see, it was designed by the East Germans, and I can tell you the building was solid. It covered about thirteen acres of land. It was one of the first of its kind, with an underground structure where the basement housed various sections—including the stores, the binding section, the letterpress section, the lightroom section, and the printing area.

Was there a design department?

Yes, there was a design department under the publishing division. When someone wanted to publish something, they would bring their material, and the publishers would work with the artists and printing press. Everything was well coordinated and ran smoothly.

Would anyone still have the architectural plans or drawings of the space?

I'm sure by now they've all been lost, possibly even destroyed. We stored them within the building itself. There was a maintenance section, and sometimes, if repairs were needed, we'd refer to those plans. But once the property was sold . . .

Enquiries we have made so far reveal that what remained of the Tema Press building was burned down some years ago. How true is this?

No, it was actually pulled down. The building was demolished and then sold. Unfortunately, many of the details surrounding the situation are unclear, so it's something that can only really be discussed at a superficial level. What I heard was that it was the warehouse of the printing press that

Ich nehme an, als staatliche Einrichtung mussten Sie die offiziellen Kanäle nutzen und sich streng an die vorgeschriebenen Verfahren halten.

Ja, aber wenn man gegen private Unternehmen antritt, ändert sich die Situation. Diese konnten Vergünstigungen anbieten, zum Beispiel Einladungen zum Mittagessen oder sogar Auslandsreisen oder Besuche bei den Familien. Wie hätten wir da mithalten können? Das waren die Herausforderungen, vor denen wir standen. Aber kommen wir zurück zur Tema Printing Press. Das Gebäude wurde von den Ostdeutschen entworfen, und ich kann sagen, dass es sehr solide gebaut war. Der Komplex erstreckte sich über eine Fläche von etwa 13 Hektar. Es war eines der ersten seiner Art mit einer unterirdischen Struktur, in der sich verschiedene Abteilungen befanden – Lagerräume, die Buchbinderei, die Buchdruckerei, die Dunkelkammer und der Druckbereich, um nur einige zu nennen.

Gab es eine Designabteilung?

Ja, es gab eine Designabteilung, die zum Verlag gehörte. Wenn jemand etwas veröffentlichen wollte, brachte er sein Material mit, und die Verleger arbeiteten mit den Künstlern und der Druckerei zusammen. Alles war gut koordiniert und lief reibungslos.

Besitzt noch jemand Baupläne oder Zeichnungen des Gebäudes?

Ich bin mir sicher, dass inzwischen alles verloren gegangen ist oder sogar zerstört wurde. Wir haben sie im Gebäude selbst aufbewahrt. Es gab eine Wartungsabteilung, und wenn Reparaturen anstanden, haben wir manchmal auf diese Pläne zurückgegriffen. Aber nachdem das Grundstück verkauft worden war ...

Nach unseren bisherigen Recherchen ist das Gebäude der Tema Press vor einigen Jahren niedergebrannt. Stimmt das?

Nein, das Gebäude wurde tatsächlich abgerissen und dann verkauft. Leider sind viele Einzelheiten unklar, man kann nur sehr allgemein über die Abläufe reden. Ich habe gehört, dass das Lagerhaus der Druckerei abgebrannt

got burned—after it had already been sold. But in the end, the whole place was demolished. You can't even find a trace of it now.

What happened to the printing machines and other equipment that were in the facility when it was sold off?

They were scrapped. Even during my time, most of the machines were already outdated. They had been installed back in the 1960s—and given how rapidly technology advances, they'd become obsolete. That, coupled with a lack of proper funding, made it difficult to keep them in working order. In the '60s, Germany was the leader in printing technology, so that's where our machines came from. But these days, if you're looking to buy printing machines, you'd most likely turn to Japan or China. It also became increasingly difficult to maintain the old machines—we just couldn't keep up.

Interesting . . . so what are some of the factors that led to its demise?

At one point, workers' salaries couldn't even be paid. Jobs weren't coming in, and we couldn't rehabilitate or upgrade the machines because of

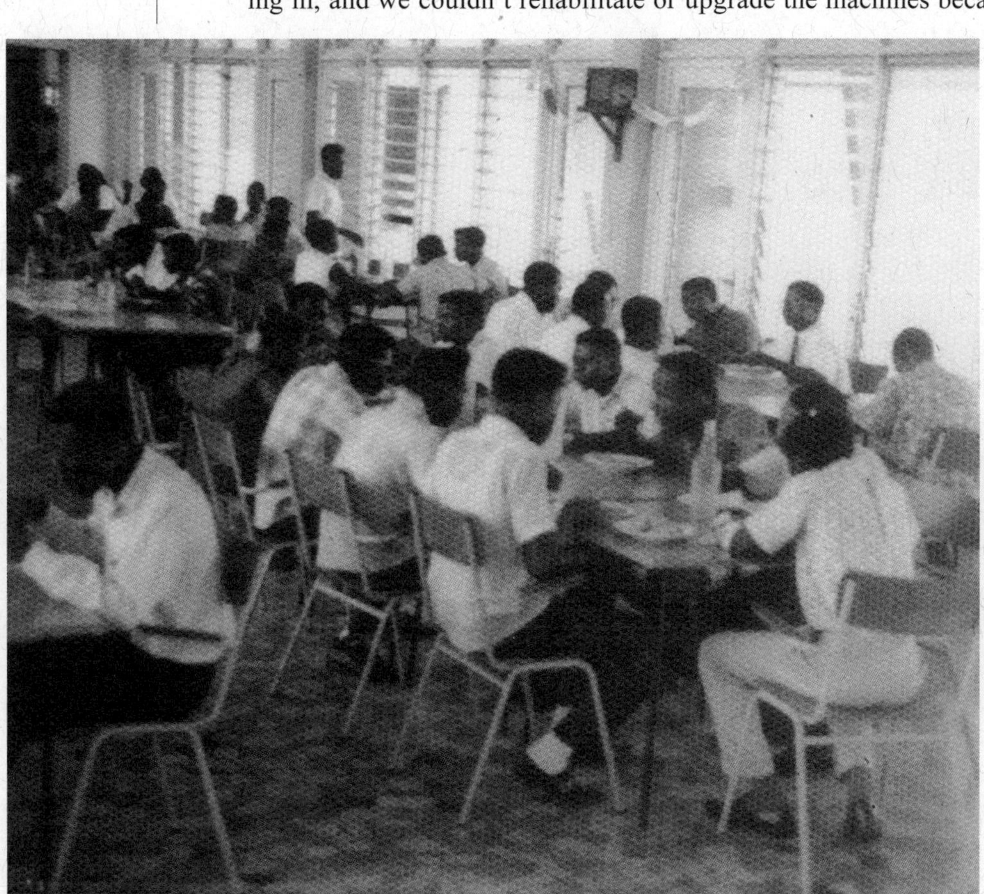

Tema in twenty-four hours (State Publishing Corporation Canteen), February 6, 1968. Photo by Paul Anane

Tema in 24 Stunden (Kantine der Staatlichen Verlagsgesellschaft), 6. Februar 1968. Foto von Paul Anane

ist, nachdem es bereits verkauft worden war. Aber letztendlich wurde die gesamte Anlage abgerissen. Heute findet man dort keinerlei Spuren mehr.

Was ist mit den Druckmaschinen und anderen Geräten passiert, die sich zum Zeitpunkt des Verkaufs in der Anlage befanden?

Sie wurden verschrottet. Selbst zu meiner Zeit waren die meisten Maschinen bereits veraltet. Sie waren in den 1960er Jahren installiert worden. Angesichts des rasanten technologischen Fortschritts waren sie längst überholt. Hinzukam, dass es an finanziellen Mitteln mangelte, um sie in einem funktionsfähigen Zustand zu halten. In den 1960er Jahren war Deutschland führend in der Drucktechnik. Von dort stammten auch unsere Maschinen. Wenn man heute Druckmaschinen kaufen möchte, wendet man sich höchstwahrscheinlich an Japan oder China. Außerdem wurde es immer schwieriger, die alten Maschinen zu warten – wir konnten einfach nicht mehr mithalten.

Interessant ... Welche Faktoren haben zum Niedergang geführt?

Irgendwann konnten wir nicht einmal mehr die Gehälter der Mitarbeitenden bezahlen. Es gab keine Aufträge mehr. Aufgrund der chronischen

chronic underfunding from the government. Even the books—our main target market—were no longer being directed our way. So, really, the decline of Ghana Publishing was gradual, but the key factors were underfunding and lack of investment. Modern printing machines were coming onto the market, but we didn't have the financial capacity to buy them, and we couldn't get the necessary approvals to make those purchases. So, over time, we ended up phasing ourselves out.

Thank you, Mr. Bekoe-Dawson, for your time and for sharing your perspective on the history of Tema Printing Press.

Unterfinanzierung durch die Regierung konnten wir die Maschinen weder sanieren noch modernisieren. Selbst Bücher – unser wichtigstes Produkt – wurden nicht mehr bei uns angefragt. Der Niedergang von Ghana Publishing verlief also schrittweise, aber die Hauptfaktoren waren die Unterfinanzierung und fehlende Investitionen. Moderne Druckmaschinen kamen auf den Markt, aber wir hatten nicht die finanziellen Mittel, sie zu kaufen. Wir konnten die notwendigen Genehmigungen für diese Anschaffungen nicht erhalten. So kam es, dass wir uns im Laufe der Zeit selbst aus dem Markt zurückgezogen haben.

Vielen Dank, Herr Bekoe-Dawson, für Ihre Zeit und dafür, dass Sie uns Ihre Sicht auf die Geschichte der Tema Printing Press geschildert haben.

ATO ANNAN is an artist, curator, and researcher based in Accra, Ghana. His work explores the complexities of history through expanded notions of archival research. His practice delves into the entangled relationship between the layers of our collective past and the present, critically examining power structures, uncovering hidden narratives, and amplifying silenced voices. Working across installations, paintings, collages, drawings, sculptures, text, sound, moving images, and public talks, he seeks to bring historical perspectives into dialogue with contemporary issues.

KONRAD HELBIG was born in 1917 in Leipzig and moved in 1946 to Mainz (later West Germany), where he passed away in 1986. He was a German photographer, art historian, and archaeologist. His photographic work is held in the Archiv der Fotografen at the Deutsche Fotothek in Dresden, in the Bildarchiv Foto Marburg at Marburg University, as well as in the Hamburg State Archive within the holdings of the German Society for Photography. His collection of photographs of male nudes is housed in the F. C. Gundlach Foundation in Hamburg.

DOREEN MENDE, PhD, has been director of the cross-collections research department of Staatliche Kunstsammlungen Dresden since 2021, associate professor of the Curatorial/Politics seminar in the Visual Arts Department at HEAD Geneva, Switzerland, since 2015, and co-founding director of the Harun Farocki Institut in Berlin.

KWASI OHENE-AYEH, PhD, is a curator and critic based in Kumasi, Ghana. He is a key member of blaxTARLINES KUMASI, whose work is inspired by the radical hope of "transforming art from commodity to gift." Ohene-Ayeh's criticism and curatorial work often explore themes such as emancipatory politics, universality, and the intersection between curatorship and pedagogy. He is a teacher in the Department of Painting and Sculpture at Kwame Nkrumah University of Science and Technology (KNUST) in Kumasi.

ATO ANNAN lebt und arbeitet als Künstler, Kurator und Forscher in Accra, Ghana. Er erforscht geschichtliche Komplexitäten, wobei seine Arbeiten von einem erweiterten Verständnis von Archiv und Recherche ausgehen. Er unternimmt Tiefenbohrungen in die verflochtenen Beziehungen zwischen den Schichten unserer kollektiven Vergangenheit und Gegenwart, untersucht kritisch Machstrukturen durch die Aufdeckung versteckter Narrative und verleiht zum Schweigen gebrachten Stimmen Nachdruck. Er arbeitet mit Installationen, Malerei, Collagen, Zeichnungen, Skulpturen, Texten, Klängen, Bewegtbildern und öffentlichen Vorträgen, um historische Perspektiven und aktuelle Themen dialogisch zusammenzuführen.

Konrad Helbig wurde 1917 in Leipzig geboren, siedelte um 1946 nach Mainz über (später Bundesrepublik Deutschland), wo er 1986 verstarb. Er war ein deutscher Fotograf, Kunsthistoriker und Archäologe. Sein fotografische Werk ist im Archiv der Fotografen in der Deutschen Fothothek Dresden, im Bildarchiv Foto Marburg der Philipps-Universität Marburg sowie im Staatsarchiv Hamburg innerhalb des Bestands der „Deutschen Gesellschaft für Photographie" archiviert. Sein Nachlass von Fotografien männlicher Akte befindet sich in der Stiftung F. C. Gundlach Hamburg.

DOREEN MENDE, PhD, ist seit 2021 Leiterin der sammlungsübergreifenden Forschungsabteilung der Staatlichen Kunstsammlungen Dresden, seit 2015 außerordentliche Professorin für Curatorial/Politics am Department Kunst der HEAD in Genf (Schweiz) sowie Mitgründerin des Harun Farocki Instituts in Berlin.

KWASI OHENE-AYEH, PhD, lebt und arbeitet als Kurator und Kritiker in Kumasi, Ghana. Er ist ein führendes Mitglied von blaxTARLINES KUMASI. Seine Arbeit ist getragen von der radikalen Hoffnung, „die Kunst von einer Ware in ein Geschenk zu verwandeln". Ohene-Ayeh widmet sich in seiner Arbeit als Kritiker und Kurator häufig Themen wie emanzipatorischer Politik, Universalität und den Schnittstellen zwischen Kuratieren und Pädagogik. Er unterrichtet am Fachbereich Malerei und Skulptur an der Kwame Nkrumah University of Science and Technology (KNUST) in Kumasi.

pp. 13–15: © Public Records and Archives Administration Department, Ghana. Photo by Ato Annan.

pp. 17–18: © Public Records and Archives Administration Department, Ghana. Photo by Ato Annan

pp. 19–21: © Public Records and Archives Administration Department, Ghana. Photo by Ato Annan

p. 22: © Photo Department of the Information Service Department, Ghana

p. 24: © Public Records and Archives Administration Department, Ghana. Photo by Ato Annan

p. 25: © Public Records and Archives Administration Department, Ghana. Photo by Ato Annan

pp. 30–32: © Ato Annan

pp. 33–34: Courtesy of Staatliche Kunstsammlungen Dresden (SKD) Münzkabinett. © Ato Annan

p. 37: Data record 71435095. © Deutsche Fotothek / Konrad Helbig

pp. 38–39: Data record 71482695. © Deutsche Fotothek / Konrad Helbig

p. 40: Data record 71482694 © Deutsche Fotothek / Konrad Helbig

p. 41: Data record 71482677. © Deutsche Fotothek / Konrad Helbig

pp. 42–43: Data record 71482691. © Deutsche Fotothek / Konrad Helbig

p. 44: Data record 71435060. © Deutsche Fotothek / Konrad Helbig

p. 45: Data record 71435062. © Deutsche Fotothek / Konrad Helbig

pp. 46–47: Data record 71435071. © Deutsche Fotothek / Konrad Helbig

p. 48: Data record 71494970. © Deutsche Fotothek / Konrad Helbig

pp. 65, 66, 68: © Information Services Department (ISD), Ghana

S. 13–15: © Public Records and Archives Administration Department, Ghana, Foto: Ato Annan

S. 17–18: © Public Records and Archives Administration Department, Ghana, Foto: Ato Annan

S. 19–21: © Public Records and Archives Administration Department, Ghana, Foto: Ato Annan

S. 22: © Photo Department of the Information Service Department, Ghana

S. 24: © Public Records and Archives Administration Department, Ghana, Foto: Ato Annan

S. 25: © Public Records and Archives Administration Department, Ghana, Foto: Ato Annan

S. 30–32: © Ato Annan

S. 33–34: Courtesy: Staatliche Kunstsammlungen Dresden (SKD), Münzkabinett, © Ato Annan

S. 37: Datensatz 71435095, © Deutsche Fotothek / Konrad Helbig

S. 38–39: Datensatz 71482695, © Deutsche Fotothek / Konrad Helbig

S. 40: Datensatz 71482694, © Deutsche Fotothek / Konrad Helbig

S. 41: Datensatz 71482677, © Deutsche Fotothek / Konrad Helbig

S. 42–43: Datensatz 71482691, © Deutsche Fotothek / Konrad Helbig

S. 44: Datensatz 71435060, © Deutsche Fotothek / Konrad Helbig

S. 45: Datensatz 71435062, © Deutsche Fotothek / Konrad Helbig

S. 46–47: Datensatz 71435071, © Deutsche Fotothek / Konrad Helbig

S. 48: Datensatz 71494970, © Deutsche Fotothek / Konrad Helbig

S. 65, 66, 68: Informationsdienstabteilung (ISD), Ghana